TES Guide to School Management

TES Guide to School Management

Gerald Haigh

Series Advisor: Bob Doe

Butterworth-Heinemann
Linacre House, Jordan Hill, Oxford OX2 8DP
A division of Reed Educational and Professional Publishing Ltd

A member of Reed Elsevier plc Group

OXFORD BOSTON JOHANNESBURG
MELBOURNE NEW DELHI SINGAPORE

First published 1997

British Library Cataloguing in Publication Data

Haigh, Gerald
  TES guide to school management
  1. School management and organization – Great Britain
  I. Title   II. Guide to school management   III. The Times
  Educational Supplement
  371.2'006

ISBN 0 7506 2800 6

Typeset by RefineCatch Limited, Bungay, Suffolk
Printed and bound in Great Britain by
Biddles Ltd, Guildford and King's Lynn

Contents

Introduction

Teachers were slow to accept the word 'management'. Management, surely, was to do with ruthless efficiency in the making of products – more and better cans of beans, at less and less cost per can. Teaching, they said, is not like that. Teaching is to do with values and emotions and attitudes and commitment. Examine a school as carefully as you like, for instance, and you will be hard pressed even to define what is its 'product'.

Gradually, though, teachers have come to realize that there are large areas of their work where it is certainly appropriate to talk about management. In many senses, indeed, teachers have always been good managers. Look at a reception teacher, responsible for the progress of thirty-five small children, all learning at different rates, all with different abilities and contrasting needs. This teacher will be handling resources and record keeping, and also supervising the work of other adults – teaching assistants, student teachers, volunteers. By any definition, such a teacher, in order to be successful, must deploy a range of high-order management skills.

Similarly, those who have been promoted, and run departments or year groups, or who are heads and deputy heads, must, whether they like it or not, be managers. They must know about budgeting, about the professional development of their colleagues, about methods of organization, about the efficient use of their premises, about discipline, salaries, safety, inspection and a whole lot of other areas, many of which are common across all the working world.

The articles here reflect the growing understanding that management is a word that sits perfectly comfortably in the world of school. Almost all of them appeared originally, in some form, in the *Times Educational Supplement*, most of them on the Management pages. The philosophy both of the TES management pages and of the selection of pieces for this book is that management need not be an abstract study, but should concern itself with real problems in real schools. These articles, therefore, aim to provide practical help for working heads and teachers. Some are by contributors with specialist knowledge and experience. Most are by the book's editor, Gerald Haigh – although what Haigh does in almost every case is present and quote the views and advice of people working in schools. The book, therefore, is a rich and unique collection of anecdotes, principles, warnings, opinions, tips and working rules all culled from people who have demonstrated that they actually work with real people and real children in real schools.

Part One
Total Quality

There is much casual use these days of the word 'quality'. Teachers and heads talk of 'quality learning experiences' and the phrase 'total quality', borrowed from the wider world of business management, is often now used in education.

But what is really under discussion here is whether schools are good at what they set out to do, and it is in this connection that teachers, parents and governors need to keep focused on what really matters.

What, after all, is the difference between a good school and a poor one? It seems an obvious question to ask, and yet it is easy to be distracted from the answer, which is that the measure of a school's quality lies in the quality of the children's learning. A good building and a distinctive uniform may win approval from parents and visitors, but they are only relevant if they have an effect on the work of children in the classroom – and the same applies, of course, to the more obviously 'educational' features such as computers, levels of corridor noise and the size of the library. Common sense suggests that a tidy school with a good library may be doing better than a school which is dirty, chaotic and under-equipped, but there is lots of middle ground, and it is the duty of governors and heads to remember always that any improvement must, eventually, earn its keep in the currency of learning.

The articles in this section deal with the quality of schooling, and look at how it might be improved. It draws heavily on the experience of schools that have made themselves more successful.

1
Total quality

The word 'quality' has crept into the workplace to the point where it can seem an almost meaningless mantra. Its origins, used in this way, can probably be traced back to the concept of 'Total Quality Management'. The guru of TQM was the late W. Edwards Deming, a management consultant who is credited with, no less, having driven the postwar rebirth of the Japanese economy. His name is revered in that country.

In the West, Deming and his methods have many devotees. For a number of reasons, his ideas appeal to educators. Here, Gerald Haigh looks at the work of people who are putting Deming's theories to work in school.

The name of W. Edwards Deming is becoming more familiar to heads and teachers, although it is still more likely than not to provoke a 'Who he?' response.

Nothing, though, is more likely to nudge educators into finding out more than the realization that, in the words of educational consultant John Marsh, 'Dr Deming's teachings make a nonsense of grading, league tables, performance related pay, etc.' And, importantly, this is not a knee-jerk ideological response, because 'He deduces this from a technical point of view, not a political one' (quoted in Malcom Greenwood and Helen Gaunt's *Total Quality Management for Schools*).

In other words it is not that league tables and the rest are immoral, or sociologically unsound, or unfair, or right wing, but that they simply do not work.

Deming, who was born in 1902 and was still hard at work until just before he died in 1995, developed his principles from a deep understanding of statistics, and honed them on forty years of experience as an internationally successful management consultant. He is generally given credit for the postwar revival of Japanese industry and since then his ideas have gradually gained ground in the West. His supporters would say that this progress has happened in line with the demonstrable failure of more aggressive, 'scientific' management methods.

The strength of Deming's philosophy comes from the rigour of its statistical foundation. Briefly, Deming says that in any system there will be a range of differences of performance. Some of these differences ('variance') are due to identifiable 'special' causes (illness, perhaps). Deming used statistical analysis to differentiate between common and special causes. Special causes are dealt with individually. What you are left with are what he called common causes.

The key is to realize that these common causes are endemic in the system. Thus the people in charge cannot get rid of them by inspecting the product and then rewarding or penalizing individuals or groups accordingly. What they must do is enlist the support of the workers in improving the system. Two of Deming's central 'Fourteen Points' are 'Cease dependence on mass inspection' and 'Remove barriers to pride of workmanship'.

Deming's supporters in education would say that you cannot improve schools by inspection, reward and punishment. The only way forward is to enlist the people who work in schools in improving them, and remove barriers to professional pride. The aim is to hone quality and get things right first time, thus making mass external inspection unnecessary. (The same analysis can apply at individual school, department and classroom levels.)

What is important to teachers about the Deming philosophy is that if you already lean towards the empowerment of teachers and pupils then Deming offers you a sound basis for your beliefs. You no longer have to rely on a vague feeling that you are probably right.

That the Deming approach 'validates' and provides intellectual support for ideas already held, sometimes in half-formed ways, was confirmed by Steven Bacon, deputy head of Matthew Moss High School in Rochdale: 'I was doing an MA, and part of the course was on Deming. When I described it to Andy Raymer (the head) we realized that was the way the school was set up. Straight away it gave us the security that we were not alone and that this was something that worked on an international scale.'

Very important to Andy Raymer is Deming's insistence on 'pride in workmanship'.

'I had always assumed that people come to work wanting to do a good job, and I thought it was because I'm an optimist. Deming says it's much more than that.'

Knowing this enables him to deal with the notion that people need to be watched, checked and penalized into working properly. 'The assumption that people don't want to do a good job is deeply insulting and demotivating, but it's also clearly wrong.'

An example of Deming in action at Matthew Moss is the school's 'Boys are Bright' project, which is intended through a series of curriculum and industry-linked initiatives to raise the aspirations of under-achieving Key Stage 3 boys. Andy Raymer says that in many cases where such potential failure is identified, 'The temptation is to blame someone – it's idleness and stupidity. Or it's poverty, or the teachers, or the England cricket team. A traditional answer would be lean on them, get tough, work them harder, give them extra homework. But what kids need to do well is self-respect, and some organizational skills, some knowledge of what to do.'

(The link between this anecdote and Deming's ideas on reducing variance through improving the system rather than through exhortation or leaning on individuals is obvious.)

There is no doubt that Matthew Moss can hit conventional targets, as the school's good OFSTED report testifies. The quality of student learning was found to be 'satisfactory or better' in nearly ninety per cent of lessons, and inspectors commented that 'Pupils show high levels of confidence and articulateness (*sic*). They respond positively to opportunities given to them in lessons to undertake a high degree of responsibility for their own learning.'

All the same, the inspectors did have difficulty in making some Matthew Moss methods fit the criteria. The school has no job descriptions, for instance, because what matters to the Deming-based institution is continuous improvement, and this means that meeting a fixed specification is a limiting concept.

Andy Raymer recalled that the inspectors wondered 'How do people know what they are supposed to do if it's not written down? We suggested they ask them, and they found that staff actually do understand.'

Staff used the inspectors' comments on behaviour and good

manners to reinforce this point. 'All teachers take responsibility for this. It's not the stuff of a job description.'

Voicing the thoughts of many heads, Andy Raymer feels that 'OFSTED works on the assumption that it's a quick fix. It is not about a process of continuous improvement.' What is important to him, though, is that Deming offers a viable alternative view.

'If anyone wants convincing I suggest they go through an OFSTED inspection and then read Deming – not the other way round, because that would be depressing.'

Above all, perhaps, Andy Raymer feels that Matthew Moss is now well equipped to meet change. Any idea that post-Dearing there is going to be a 'breathing space' is mistaken, he believes. He contrasts 'the belief that things will return to some notion of normality' with 'the absolute certainty that things will continue to move'.

Now, though, 'We can move faster than anything the government can throw at us.'

British Deming Association, The Old George Brewery
Rollastone Street, Salisbury SP1 1DX

2

Aims statements

Does your school have an aims statement? Does it actually mean anything? Is it likely to have an effect on the quality of teaching and learning in the school? Gerald Haigh here looks at some research into the nature of school aims statements.

Just about every school these days has an agreed statement of its aims. Competition for pupils, the requirement to produce development plans and the advent of teacher appraisal have all combined to persuade teachers and governors of the need to write something purposeful for the staff handbook or the prospectus.

To what extent, though, does a carefully crafted public statement provide a real and practical focus for the work of a school? Or is it naive even to expect it to have that sort of purpose? Those who suspect that aims statements are often nothing more than verbal blazer badges will be interested in a small-scale research project, 'What are Schools For?', which was carried out by Peter Batty and Clive Carroll at Lancaster University's Charlotte Mason In-Service Development Unit.

The project looked at the stated aims of forty-one secondary schools in two contrasting authorities – Cumbria and Rochdale. The chief characteristic, it seems, was a great variation in both content and style. One school, for example, had its eighteen aims set out in a fifteen-page A5 booklet. Another had but one aim, handwritten by the head. Most commonly, there were one or two sides of A4, although even within this format there were wide differences – some schools had lists of aims; others had one general aims statement supported by subheadings.

The central problem, clearly, was a lack of agreement about the basic concept. 'There was,' said the research report, 'a lot of inconsistency in the way schools interpret the word "aims", often bordering on and occasionally descending into confusion.'

One school, for example, made no clear distinction between values and aims, and another, having set out five 'beliefs', then went on to refer to them as 'objectives'.

Nevertheless, the researchers did succeed in dividing aims into two types: 'Those concerned with (or phrased in terms of) what the school could provide, and those concerned with (or phrased in terms of) pupil outcomes'.

Among the statements which focused on school provision, the most common strands were to do with 'the kind of learning and caring environment which a school sought to provide as well as its broad and balanced curriculum, often extending beyond the classroom door'. This kind of document often spoke of 'excellence and high standards'. Another common concept was that of partnership – although, says the research report, 'Partnership is rarely defined in any practical sense.'

A few schools offered something more idiosyncratic. One wanted only 'To be recognized as the best secondary school in the area'.

More surprisingly, perhaps, although a fair number of schools wanted education to be seen as a lifelong process, only three set out to put secondary education in the context of the 3–18 continuum.

Those statements which were centred around pupil outcomes tended to deal with the notion that school is a preparation for life, and included themes such as 'achieving potential, having individual needs met, and developing awareness of self in relation to others'.

What was most obviously missing, though, was an explicit intention that pupils be enabled to take advantage of the opportunities which are offered. Only two schools made reference to this – one, for example, says, 'It is not enough that such an entitlement (to a broad and balanced curriculum) should be offered: it must be organized in such a way that each student is encouraged to take up their opportunity.'

This absence of focus on the learning of individual pupils reflects the concern which the Teachers' Pay Review Body expressed in its 1995 report: 'Important management weaknesses . . . include . . . a failure to focus sufficiently on pupils' achievements, on outcomes as well as processes.'

Of course it could be argued – and instinctively you feel it would be true – that the schools whose aims consist of generalities are probably just as pedagogically effective as those which define more specific outcomes.

This, though, simply raises the question of what aims statements are for. Is the process of writing them, asked Clive Carroll, 'a bureaucratic activity or a professional one? Are they for an outside audience, or do they provide something for people to live by?'

Thus, in concluding their report, Carroll and Batty listed the questions that their work had thrown up – who, for example, writes the school's aims, and for what audience? To what extent does the wider school community identify with the published aims, and how is school life influenced by them? And perhaps most important of all, 'How often and in what way are a school's aims honestly and openly reviewed?'

Checklist

- Keep the aims statement long enough to say something, but not so long that it becomes a sermon. A side of A4 seems reasonable.
- Avoid meaningless slogans. The aims should relate to the main purpose of the school, which is to promote learning.
- Be clear about the audience.
- Pupils, staff, governors and parents should understand the aims and generally agree with them.

3
Preparing for inspection

There have always been school inspectors – Her Majesty's Inspectors of Schools have been with us since the beginning of state education. Government philosophy in the late 1980s, however, was that the system needed more rigour, and should be less influenced by the views of the teachers themselves. Thus was created the Office for Standards in Education, committed to a regular programme of school inspection according to a published framework, with public results and clear messages about success and failure.

This has caused schools to consider how they might prepare themselves for inspection. Here Gerald Haigh looks at the experience of some successful primary schools.

Given the amount of concern that there is among teachers and governors still awaiting the attention of OFSTED, it struck me that one way to help them would be to approach primary heads whose schools had been inspected in the first round and ask them how they prepared.

In each case I sought out schools which had won high praise, on the assumption that a good inspection report presupposes good preparation. Key phrases in these schools' reports included 'effective leadership and management', 'well led, well organized', 'teachers have high expectations at all times', 'there are no major issues for this very good school to address'. Each was quietly, yet deeply and obviously proud that its qualities had been publicly endorsed.

It soon became clear that there is no standard route to OFSTED success. Take, for example, the question of whether or not you should seek local authority help. Lesley Broady, of Oakwood Junior in Warrington, was one head who took everything that Cheshire had to offer. 'I attended all the courses, residential and non-residential, and we invited the primary adviser, and others from the authority, to talk to us and answer our questions.'

And similarly, Pam Williamson of Stapely Broad Lane C of E primary in Crewe 'went on a lot of authority courses. I couldn't have done without them.' Cheshire primary heads, in fact, are particularly complimentary about the unassertive pre-inspection support given by their authority advisers. Meetings with fellow heads either facing inspection or looking back on it were also mentioned as useful by several of those to whom I spoke.

A couple of hundred miles south, however, in Gosport, Anne Cousins of Alverstoke Infants – although she works routinely with Hampshire advisers – was quite sure that she wanted nobody in to tell her specifically about OFSTED. 'We very consciously had none of that. I didn't want the nervousness increased. We had to be confident about what we were doing and we didn't want somebody saying we should do something different.'

Ray Sharp, for twenty-three years head of Hartford Manor Primary in Northwich, also had a healthy scepticism about courses. 'I think a lot of them have been designed to put the fear of God into people.'

(Ray Sharp, incidentally, famously remonstrated with the inspectors for being too ready to use the word 'outstanding' in describing a particular curriculum area. 'I said I didn't think it was. They told me I didn't see what they saw.')

Another difference was that between schools which prepared in detail a long time in advance and others where some last-minute scurrying took place. Thus Pam Williams had a Governors OFSTED Committee as soon as OFSTED was set up, and long before they had an inspection date. 'We sent questionnaires to parents in the same style as OFSTED; we talked to parents about it at the annual meeting.'

Lesley Broady, too, had taken a long run at it. 'All our policies were dated from five years ago, and it had obviously been a gradual process.'

Other heads worked from scratch when the letter arrived – often because, like Paul Makin of Little Sutton C of E Primary in Ellesmere Port, they had only just been appointed. 'I started on the Monday and the envelope came on the Friday.'

There were some advantages in this, however. Not only did the prospect of OFSTED give him, as a new head, a clear developmental focus, but 'it helped me to get to know systems, people and policies in the authority quicker than I would otherwise have done'.

Paul Makin's approach, therefore – he had a year's notice – was intense and highly organized. 'The run-up got increasingly more rigorous but we paced it to keep things in perspective.'

He was very careful to involve everyone. There were a number of working parties involving governors and parents, for example. He made sure that none of this committee work was lost: 'I found I was minuting everything – every minor meeting and working party. I was aware all the time that I needed evidence.'

Ray Sharp makes no bones about the fact that virtually all of his paperwork was put together in the lead-up to the inspection. 'Prior to that I had no schemes of work, and I quickly had to get some.' His own speciality is maths, which he himself teaches throughout the upper part of the school. 'But I had no scheme. I did one on the beach in Greece. It had suntan oil all over it.'

It needs to be said, though, that what Ray Sharp and his colleagues did was not to create fantasy schemes, but to write down and describe work which he already believed to be of high quality. He also became convinced that the documentation exercise was not only worth while, but 'the best thing I've ever done'.

Vive, you might say, *les différences*. But when you look closely, you start to see that these able heads have a number of qualities in common.

The most obvious is that of confidence – the kind of quietly self-assured approach that rubs off on staff and pupils. 'You have to have confidence in your school', said Anne Cousins. And Pam Williamson, too, felt that 'If you think you are doing your best for the children you must have faith.'

Importantly, in each of these schools, priority was given to using this confidence to keep up staffroom morale. 'The nearer it got to the day,' recalled Lesley Broady, 'the more it became very much a supportive thing for me. I provided time before and after school to talk to them individually and in groups, to make sure we were keeping on line and not being sidetracked through anxiety.'

Another aspect of pre-inspection confidence lies in having proper priorities. Malcolm Lee, head of Halfway Infants in Sheffield, spoke for all of the heads when he suggested that 'The school development plan was crucial.' He made the point that if the development plan is clear, then it removes the need to be hurtling about trying to do everything at once. 'Even if some things are not in place, the SDP indicates the areas you have identified for attention.'

Each head agreed that in any case there is little point in last-minute panic, because the inspectors are simply not going to be taken in. 'We didn't change our teaching styles – they'd have soon seen through all that,' said Rosemary Sadler of Belchamp St Paul C of E Primary in Essex.

By the same token, the experience is that inspectors do, by and large, see through to the 'hidden' areas of pride that so many heads feel might be missed. Thus Rosemary Sadler was pleased that 'They soon picked up on the ethos of the school – that the older children cared for the younger ones, for example.'

At the same time, the heads suggest that you have to be ready to steer the inspectors towards the good things. Pam Williamson said that she 'made a point all week of saying to them "Do you realize this – did you know that". You've got to blow your own trumpet.'

The message of these schools, then, is that the best route to a good inspection report is through self-confidence based on purpose and quality in the classroom and good forward planning. By contrast, last-minute application of gloss, with the creation of drifts of documents unsubstantiated by practice, is not only a waste of time but is counter-productive.

Chris Woodhead, when I talked through these issues with him, was at pains to bring the same message to heads and governors.

'I think that good schools are likely simply to get on with their day-to-day business. There is nothing to be gained by trying to get every policy document that's possible shaped and polished in some definitive version.'

It is a view which leads him to be doubtful about the pre-inspection (and post-inspection) growth industry of consultancy, and to suggest that the roots of school improvement lie primarily within the institution itself. 'External support may or may not be necessary but it is not of the same order.'

He worries, therefore, about the activities of those local authorities that apply a standard pre-OFSTED 'MOT' to every school due for inspection.

'I'm not saying support shouldn't be there for those who want it, but to work on the assumption that every school has to have the same amount of help is wrong. Those authorities that approach it in too bureaucratic a manner result in greater anxiety than there was before. I think it's wrong for authorities to pander to the insecurities of schools.'

The good news, finally, from the heads to whom I spoke, is that preparation is the hard part. The experience itself can actually be quite pleasant.

Ray Sharp, for instance, who worried a little that he might 'get some flak' for his very hands-on management style, found them 'nice people, very professional and thorough. I was teaching all the time they were here and I used to enjoy them coming to watch me.'

And Malcolm Lee thought that 'the team carried out the inspection very well. As the week went on we all felt very positive and, dare I say, started to enjoy it!'

Checklist

- Get paperwork up to date, but make sure it describes reality – the inspectors will check that it does, by talking to pupils as well as to teachers.
- Use the updating process as a tool to improve the practice.
- Do not spend valuable time on what are obviously cosmetic changes.
- Protect the staff from unnecessary worry.
- Have confidence in your own proved practice.
- Use outside help only as and when you need it, to suit your own agenda – do not swamp staff with preparatory visits or 'pre-inspections'.
- Direct the inspectors to the things you do not want them to miss.

4

Investors in people

Schools are searching for ways both of improving their own performance and also of demonstrating that commitment to the outside world. One way of doing this is to gain the Investors in People Award. Often thought of as a scheme for business and industry, this is in fact suitable for just about any organization that employs people, and schools are becoming increasingly interested in it.

Sarah Farley reports on how the Investors in People scheme has helped one primary school recognize its strengths.

'If I had thought of it first, I would have called my own philosophy Investors in People,' said Linda Murphy, headteacher of Endike Primary School, Hull. Instead her school, with 40 staff and 400 pupils, mostly from the North Hull Estate, was the first primary to be recognized by the training and enterprise councils as having achieved the Investors in People standard.

Launched in 1993, Investors in People aims to help organizations of all kinds improve their performance by releasing the full potential of their workforces. Businesses that have achieved the standard range from well-known retailers, such as Sainsbury and WH Smith, to small family firms. Non-commercial organizations are also recognized, such as Braintree District Council, but the fastest growing area of interest is from schools.

To begin with it was secondaries that took the lead. Now, though, many primaries have achieved the standard or are at the initial stage of commitment.

Linda Murphy's interest in Investors in People began after she and her school came top in the staff development category of a Humberside business award. 'The more I discovered about it, the more it seemed to fit in with my ideas for managing a school. As I read through the requirements, I realized we already had many structures in place, such as the school management plan and the appraisal system.

'I believe very strongly that it is the people working in the school that give it its strength,' she says. 'They should be encouraged and enabled to make the most of their abilities. I am not just talking about the teaching staff; opportunities to develop and contribute should be available to everyone connected with the school.'

All the staff unanimously agreed that the school should commit itself to Investors in People. Then a member of Humberside TEC spoke to the governors about what was involved but left them unconvinced. 'As all previous presentations had been to businesses, it seemed too business orientated and some governors felt it would be irrelevant to us,' says Linda Murphy. 'Because I was convinced it was the right thing, I had to re-present it, explaining the value I thought it would have.'

The next stage was for Linda Murphy to meet her mentor, Alan Challis, from Humberside TEC. He provided her with a tool kit, including information about the national standard and its links to assessment indicators, a brief for top managers, and a survey entitled 'How do we measure up?' The last was circulated to all staff and in the 100 per cent return, Linda Murphy and Alan Challis were able to identify three areas that needed attention for the school to meet the standard:

- an induction programme for new employees and those changing their job in the school;
- an induction programme for student teachers;
- improvement of draft job descriptions.

Having established it was feasible to apply for the standard, the school had to make a public and formal commitment and display a plaque showing its intent. At this stage, Linda Murphy made two personal commitments to the scheme, undertaking to collate the portfolio of evidence that would be presented to the assessors, and to find a sponsor for the £500 required for the assessment fee.

The latter proved elusive up until the eleventh hour but Linda Murphy now maintains that the value of the exercise was such that she would not hesitate to fund it from the school budget. The fee varies from TEC to TEC and some areas help by paying for pre-assessment before commitment.

Originally it was thought that the three points raised could be cleared in three months, but the discussions proved so useful that the time limit was extended and it took a year from commitment to achieving the standard. Improving the induction programme involved Linda Murphy in a teacher placement with Marks and Spencer in Hull, learning about the firm's induction scheme. The result of this and other ideas is a programme that offers new staff more support while involving current staff.

For example, a new member of staff has health, safety and fire procedures explained by the caretaker on a tour of the school. They are also assigned a mentor to help them settle in to the school's routines. The job descriptions have been rewritten after consultation with the staff and are now in place ready for when the school is required to present them.

Six-monthly meetings with Alan Challis helped Linda Murphy become clear in her own mind about how to link the aims and objectives of the management plan, and so to make them clearer for her staff too. Collecting evidence for the assessors, she referred to the twenty-four assessment indicators provided by Investors in People, which were divided into commitment, planning, action and evaluation.

'Evaluation was the most difficult. If your business is producing cans, you can quantify production and work out personnel efficiency, but with children the true evidence might not come out until they themselves are parents. But when I looked at, for example, "the organization evaluates how its development of people is contributing to business goals and targets", I realized I could meet it by such information as our observation of children and their work, by the reviews for governors, appraisal, training and the weekly lesson plan.'

The assessor's visit, a full day, involved fourteen members of staff, some new, some established, teaching and non-teaching. The reports that filtered back showed that the staff endorse the school's commitment to the scheme and are supportive of Linda Murphy's management.

Maggie Morris, special needs co-ordinator and Year 4 and 5 teacher, was one of the teachers interviewed by the assessor. 'Filling in the questionnaires about how the school worked made me think more about what I do.'

Year 6 teacher and group leader, Lynne Stratton, comments: 'It involved us in very little extra work because we were already carrying out the actions and responsibilities through the existing school management. Any changes have just helped to make the school run even more smoothly.'

An added bonus of achieving the Investors in People standard is that many of the requirements overlap those needed for an OFSTED inspection. 'We already have most of the information in place, but as we have to keep updating our material for Investors in People, and a second assessment in three years' time, we will be ready when we have an inspection.'

But what matters more to Linda Murphy is the achievement the standard represents: 'We have a plan we constructed for Endike school and we have made a good team better'.

Details of the Investors in People Scheme are available from local Training and Enterprise Councils.

5
School improvement 1

School improvement – school effectiveness. Both phrases can be little more than slogans unless heads and teachers give real thought to what they mean in their own institutions. In particular, they have to consider how the two words 'effectiveness' and 'improvement' can be focused on the point where learning takes place – in the classroom, at the desk of the individual pupil. Here, Gerald Haigh describes a school improvement programme specifically aimed at children's learning.

In one sense, school improvement can be quick, easy and effective – a new uniform, some flower beds, a mobile phone for the head, and in no time at all the enrolment starts to rise.

By contrast, however, a programme aimed where it counts – at the point of contact between teacher and pupil – may well take a long time to show results, be difficult to explain briefly, and be relatively invisible to the casual observer. Mary Fowler, one of a number of Bradford heads involved in a school effectiveness project, finds that its flexible, long-term nature 'makes it hard to explain, because it's process based, and you don't understand it till you're doing it'.

'Effective Schools for All', the project to which Mary Fowler is referring, made use of a pack of teacher education materials ('Special Needs in the Classroom') developed by UNESCO and used in over forty countries, as well as in a number of schools across the UK. (Although the pack set out to address special needs, UK schools have taken the view that it speaks to the whole spectrum of learning.) The project starts with the assumption that 'a collaborative approach to teacher development within and between schools can lead to continued improvement in the learning experience for all children', and emphasizes that only lengthy continuous commitment will show results. 'This project is not a quick fix.'

Four schools in Bradford were engaged together for over a year in 'Effective Schools for All' with the support of a consultant employed by the authority. I visited two of them – Buttershaw First, and Heaton Royds, a special school for pupils with moderate and severe learning difficulty – with the aim of finding what it all means for heads, teachers and pupils.

One theme, I rapidly discovered, is that of partnership. In both schools, for example, teachers had begun by forming self-selected two-person partnerships. Each pair chose a focus for study and improvement – the teaching of maths, for example, or group work, or reading.

These 'areas of focus' were freely chosen, and developed without intervention from senior colleagues. The idea is that teachers should be able, in pairs, to address areas in which they consider themselves professionally insecure, without feeling themselves under the eye of management. Julie Perry, deputy head at Buttershaw, explained that 'We wanted them to feel a sense of trust and lack of interference.' (The project envisages that pairs of teachers should be able to keep confidential to themselves as much of their partnership work as they wish.)

At the same time, though, management is supportive of the partnerships in that teachers are given time, by the use of supply cover paid for from the school's INSET budget, to meet for discussion and to carry out observation of each other's classroom work.

Staff at both schools emphasized that for them, the partnerships represented much more than the usual helpfulness between colleagues. 'It might be a general truth that teachers are supportive of one another,' explained Heaton Royds teacher Tim Billingsley, 'but usually, time is not set aside for it.' And Shirley Malley, another Heaton Royds teacher, claimed that 'It's affected my classroom practice. Supportive discussion on its own might not do that.'

These partnerships, although only part of the story, have obviously been a vital ingredient in improving practice and planning in both schools. In each case, teachers have talked together, watched each other in class, and agreed on how to do things better. They have had plenty of time – a whole school year – and a minimum of pressure from above. According to Tim Billingsley, 'We've all felt that it was time well spent – and that's not always true of in-service training projects.'

The partnership theme is picked up in a number of other ways. Schools make links with each other, for example, both within Bradford and outside – thus Buttershaw has good professional contacts with a school on the Isle of Man. In the classroom, too, pupils work in pairs, working collaboratively, discussing and checking each other's work.

Another strong feature of the 'Effective Schools for All' project is that of evaluation – acceptance of the need to check that ideas and plans are turning into reality in the classroom. Heaton Royd's head, Mary Fowler, talks of 'a clear link between planning and action – tying up school goals with individual goals', and has invested a significant amount of the school's in-service training resources on evaluating the teacher partnerships and the school's involvement in the project as a whole.

At Buttershaw, too, there is awareness of the need to make things happen in the classroom. Julie Perry explains that the partnership scheme has developed into a system whereby 'Every teacher now has a checking partner to ensure we put policy into practice.'

Collaboration between schools in the project also helps to move things forward. Julie Perry explained that the project co-ordinators from the participating Bradford schools meet regularly for seminars and workshops. 'That's really important, because you agree on what's going to happen next, and then when you go back to the next meeting they ask you how it went.'

Mary Fowler, too, feels that 'Being with the project is a catalyst – there's someone there asking you questions and helping you to carry out your action plan.'

Each of these two schools is now into the second year of the project. In both cases, there has been a gradual maturing – from teacher partnerships to a perception of the need for a more unified, whole-school approach. Teachers at both schools now feel that their work is more focused, and more consistent across the staff. Buttershaw, explained Julie Perry, 'has now got a really supportive format for planning – a rolling programme for all key elements of the National Curriculum'.

Richard Lewis, who teaches a mixed Y3/Y4 class at Buttershaw, sees teachers being more willing and able to share their expertise. 'Instead of being isolated, with closed doors, we work much more as a staff now. We're happy, in a spirit of trust, to share our worries and concerns.'

All the same, I wondered, is it all – partnerships and planning – not just a lot more work for already busy teachers? Julie Perry shook her head firmly at this, and pointed out, for example, that planning documentation at Buttershaw has actually been slimmed down. 'We're not asking people to do more. We're asking that the work they do is effective.'

All the teachers agreed that no school improvement plan is worth a fig unless it improves the classroom performance of pupils. At the same time, they were very aware of the difficulty of making a sensible objective measure of progress, especially over as short a period as a year and a term. Richard Lewis pointed out that 'You can't have a control group against which other children might be measured', and Mary Fowler made the same point – 'We can't know what they'd be like if we hadn't done it.'

In the longer term, objective internal and national tests may tell the story. In the shorter term, the evidence for improvement goes something like this.

If you visibly improve the input side of the equation – if teachers work more collaboratively, helping each other to fill gaps in their professionalism; if planning is more coherent and uniform across the school; if there is increased awareness of the need for evaluation and for the concept of 'plans into action' – then it seems reasonable to assume that the performance of pupils will improve.

If, at the same time, pupils are visibly better behaved and motivated, then this makes the same assumption even more reasonable – and teachers in both schools report that pupils are spending more time 'on task'. Last term, an evaluation at Heaton Royds, for example, reported 'Children's awareness levels and involvement greatly increased; some children's powers of reasoning enhanced; children beginning to make choices about what to keep for their records of achievement.'

Tim Billingsley, at Heaton Royd, summed it up as 'Our children have more knowledge of what they are going to do and more understanding of what they have done.'

Details of 'Effective Schools for All' from the Director, Maggie Balshaw, 33 Greens Road, Cambridge CB4 3EF

6

School improvement 2

There are also many individual examples of schools where staff have succeeded in improving behaviour and academic results. Garibaldi School in Nottinghamshire captured attention in 1995 because of the obvious strides it had made in a few years under an able head teacher. Gerald Haigh describes some of the secrets of Garibaldi's success.

We all know the folktale of radical school improvement. It begins in a dank and dismal classroom peopled by illiterate arsonists and a weeping teacher. It proceeds to the arrival of a charismatic leader who grabs the scruffs of necks, inspires, infuriates and evangelizes. And it finishes in the sumptuously carpeted new resource centre, with a ceremony in which scrubbed and barbered youngsters are awarded fistfuls of certificates.

Harmless nonsense, of course – and yet, take Garibaldi School in Mansfield, dubbed 'a role model school' by David Blunkett and featured as an example of good practice by Sir John Harvey Jones in TV's 'Troubleshooter'.

Garibaldi serves the former mining villages of Clipstone and Forest Town in North Nottinghamshire, where unemployment runs at twenty per cent. In the late 1982s the school was near to the bottom of the Nottinghamshire exam league table. By 1995 it was a third of the way from the top. Then, vandalism was costing £40,000 a year. In 1995 it cost £270 for one broken window. Then, fifty pupils a year from feeder primaries were sent to other schools. By 1995 they were all coming to Garibaldi. Pupil numbers rose in that time from just over 500 to nearly 900. The sixth form went from eight students to 125. Truancy was almost completely eliminated, and attendance rates raised to ninety-eight per cent. Those are the measurable indicators. The subjective ones – the alert, positive feel of the place and the positive attitude of all its people – became equally visible.

How has it happened? The quick answer is that six and a half years ago Bob Salisbury went in and turned the place around. What colleagues across the country want to know, though, is how he actually did it – which, presumably, is why the school's television appearance produced an almost unmanageable number of requests to visit.

Bob Salisbury knew early on that he would not be able to do what he wanted through the existing conventional management pyramid, made up of deputy heads together with heads of faculties, years and departments.

'It took three months for an idea to go down through the hierarchy and then three months for it to come back up again – and in the meantime somebody had changed their mind. The plan for Records of Achievement did three laps of the circuit – and this was in a school that needed massive, instant change.'

What he had to do, he decided, was to take out layers of management and replace them with something more flexible and responsive.

'We reduced the number of deputies, took out all the heads of faculties, reduced the heads of year, and got rid of all assistant heads of everything. We scrapped all formal meetings; got rid of rules for every contingency, and above all saw the motivation and development of all staff as our greatest asset.'

To use his own imagery, the pyramid has been replaced by a 'bobbing corks' model in which, restricted only by the river banks (read 'school philosophy' here), individuals are free to rise to the surface and make their unimpeded way. Implicit in this model is the idea that some of the corks will get into difficulty. He welcomes this: 'I want a risk-taking culture in which inertia is the only crime.'

So far so good. But the alert reader will now want to know how motivating it might be to call in senior faculty heads, or assistant year heads, and tell them that their job has been phased out and that they have been transformed into bobbing corks.

Here Bob Salisbury showed most conspicuously the high quality of his leadership as he interviewed colleagues and moved them on to a new way of working, positively, and with sensitive regard to status. His aim throughout was to put flesh on his belief 'that we needed to release all the talents of the staff'.

Faculty heads, for example, became the leaders of influential review and working groups who look at areas of the curriculum and of school life – 'mini OFSTED teams', Bob Salisbury calls them. 'They've done science, maths, and the pastoral system and they're now doing art. They observe a lot of lessons, talk to a lot of pupils, a lot of staff, then come up with a kind of report that draws all that together with key issues. The report is hard-hitting and we follow up with timed targets for improvement.' (The report on Humanities, which I saw, is at least as perceptive as any OFSTED document, and very clearly focused on 'Areas for Development'.)

'Ruthless promotion of talent' is how Bob Salisbury put his way of bringing on people of ability. The way a new head of sixth form was appointed makes a good example. 'I had a teacher doing community projects. I asked him what his dream job was and he said head of sixth form. It turned out he had the clearest possible plan of how to develop a sixth form in this school, and he built it up from eight students to 120.'

Another teacher who was first doubtful and then inspired by the changes was Garibaldi's Information Technology Co-ordinator. When Bob arrived, she had been at Garibaldi for fifteen years as an English teacher and an assistant head of house. The house job disappeared under the management reorganization, and when she was unsuccessful in becoming a year head, she was disappointed. 'I was bogged down. I couldn't see where I was going.'

Then, in 1989, computers started to come into school. 'I was interested and I began to see what computers could mean to the whole of school life.'

The appraisal process picked this interest up very quickly and she found that her commitment was supported by the head and the whole team, and she became IT Co-ordinator.

'I had whatever training I wanted, and resources within reason. To say it's been a new lease of life is an understatement. It was as if my teaching career started at day one again. I've found that I have a knowledge that other people don't have and I now get the kind of feedback from pupils and colleagues that many teachers have been starved of for years.'

The word she used most often about Bob Salisbury was 'positive'.

'There's his perception of people's talents, the ease of access to him, and his willingness to let you have a go and make mistakes. And if you go to see him with an idea he doesn't want to say No. He always says, "Let's see how we can achieve that." '

The effect on pupils, she believes, has been to raise both morale and expectations. 'Girls especially now look beyond leaving school and having a family straight away.'

In fact, Bob Salisbury deliberately aims to transmit the school's responsive and flexible style to the pupils. 'In an area like ours, where traditional industries have disappeared, pupils will need over the next thirty years to become enterprising, flexible and entrepreneurial.'

Much of what the school has done in the Salisbury years has cost money. There were pressing cosmetic needs at the start – to decorate rooms and replace shredded curtains. Then, more and more plans and projects were thrown up that needed significant cash – for computers, technology equipment, language resources, outdoor facilities, sixth form accommodation. Here Bob Salisbury quickly showed that he is well equipped with yet another latter-day headship skill – that of raising money from outside sources: industry, trusts, the European Community. He has had to work assiduously at this. 'Not a single lead came into my office. We had to go out and look for the right frog to kiss.' The accuracy of his kissing may be judged by the fact that his forays into sponsorship raised £420,000 for the school in 1995.

It is within our national character to look suspiciously at success, and there will be those who want to know if there is another Garibaldi tale, about snags and difficulties and trodden-upon toes, and messy resignations. Indeed, Bob Salisbury likens the first couple of years to pushing a snowball uphill. 'But in the pushing of the snowball the crucial thing is keeping your head up and appearing confident.'

Then, however, after a couple of years came the kind of visible successes that win the support of doubters. 'The first thing was the vandalism stopped. And gradually I was pushing the snowball on the level, and then it was going downhill, gathering snow and bounding along.'

Checklist for a new head determined on improvement

- Listen with respect, but regard nothing as sacred.
- Identify hidden talents and work towards releasing them.
- Make sure the management structure is not an obstacle to quick decision making.
- Look for funding for individual high-profile projects.
- Raise pupil expectations and you raise achievement.

7

School improvement 3: Pupils with portfolio

Another route to school improvement lies through careful staff development. In this article, Kate Myers visits a very special school where everyone from the head down is regarded as a learner.

Just as pupils' achievements at Addington School, Reading, are recorded in their records of achievement, so do staff, from head to teacher assistants, use personal development portfolios to record their learning. Certificates, photographs, videos, witness testimonies and sometimes personal reflective pieces on professional practice and issues are all included.

Everything at Addington is geared to improving children's learning, with considerable emphasis on staff development and self-evaluation. Sammie Armstrong, the head, wants the school to become self-inspecting. He believes OFSTED is a necessary mechanism but that an external, summative, four-yearly report is of limited use to a school. He also thinks that the system disempowers teachers and that it's time heads, teachers and pupils took more control of what is going on.

Every teacher and teacher assistant is consequently allocated eight days every year for their professional development; one-third for their subject responsibility, one-third for personal professional development and the other third for school evaluation. A topic is chosen for evaluation and two teachers, one classroom assistant and the quality assurance manager decide how to go about this task.

Jan Beats, a curriculum co-ordinator, was involved in the first exercise which looked at speaking and listening across the curriculum. They decided to look at group work and involved colleagues by asking them to video their own practice or offering to do so for them. Jan believes that evaluation exercises where the topic is identified by the school, carried out by the staff and seen as a continuous process in-built in the system, complements inspections.

She feels the school learned a lot from the exercise (including that they need to be more specific about the focus). She values the opportunities regularly offered for her development.

Zoë Meeson has been a teacher assistant at the school for six and a half years and hopes to train as a teacher in the future. She appreciates being treated like a professional, expected to pull her weight, encouraged to go on courses and progress in her career. She likes the portfolio system and finds being part of the pilot peer appraisal scheme with another teacher assistant rewarding.

Addington focuses on pupils' attainment and assessment and emphasizes putting them in charge of their own learning. National Curriculum targets have been broken down so that progress is continually noted. In English, for instance, twenty-one different points are assessed between levels one and two. Individual targets are set for each child at an annual review and progress is assessed. Pupils are encouraged to reflect on and be proud of their achievements. Six-year-old James Trigg, about to change schools, patiently showed me the work he had helped his teacher collect to take to his new school and read me his contribution to his annual review. From an early age pupils are invited to contribute and/or attend these reviews.

Parents are seen as important partners. As well as being invited in for informal coffee mornings, each term they discuss a programme and targets with their child's tutors and agree what is appropriate to do at home.

As the pupils get older and involved in this process themselves, parents are sent the individual programmes in the core subjects, humanities, art and design, and personal and social development.

For Jeanette Nettleton, the secondary curriculum development leader, this means completing fifty-three programmes each term in her own subject of science, and twelve for her tutor group in personal and social development. It is time-consuming but the pay-off in parental support and involvement makes it well worth the effort, she says.

Eighteen-year-old Nicola Maxwell – one of Addington's 210 pupils with a wide range of learning difficulties including emotional, profound and multiple learning difficulties – proudly showed me her record of achievement portfolio which includes photos of her at her work experience placement in Shire Hall. She explained the importance of witness statements in this record and how she had gone about getting hers.

Addington's vision statement says there are 'no limits to the improvements we can bring about'. Mainstream schools could learn a lot from very special schools such as Addington.

Kate Myers is an associate director of the International School Effectiveness and Improvement Centre, Institute of Education, University of London, and co-ordinates its school improvement network.

8

Primary consortia 1

Throughout the 1990s primary schools were increasingly facing new challenges while finding at the same time that there was less and less support from their local authorities. Many of them dealt with this by forming groupings and alliances. These took different forms in response to local needs. Gerald Haigh describes two of them here. One is a grouping of three primary heads, the other a larger alliance of neighbouring schools.

There is an increasing tendency for schools in the primary sector to come together in pursuit of common problems and interests.

These groups commonly have at least a dozen or so members, partly because they are seeking economies of scale in areas such as purchasing and in-service provision.

That there may, however, be a role for much smaller groups was demonstrated by 'Triad', an alliance of three Hertfordshire primary heads – Michael Connell of St Peter's Primary in St Albans, Alisdair Skinner of Hurst Drive JMI in Waltham Cross and Martin Tuck of Fairfields JMI in Cheshunt.

'Triad' (the name started as a joke, but it stuck) is a formally defined link which enables the three heads to work together on common management problems and, importantly, to buy in the part-time support of a management consultant.

The aim, essentially, is to save management time by preventing the continuous reinvention of the wheel. Martin Tuck, head of Fairfields Primary, who had the original idea, points out that 'Primary heads receive virtually identical postbags from the authority and the DFEE and they have many identical or parallel management decisions to consider, one annual example being the setting of the school budget.'

There are other common areas too, from school brochures and

standard letters to major policies on, for example, health and safety. And even where individual schools have differing approaches, it is frequently possible to identify a basic framework that they can share. Consultant Alan Craig, who acts as part-time professional assistant to 'Triad', finds that the management concerns are so alike that 'It's difficult to see things that don't have common possibilities.'

None of this, in principle, will be news to the average primary head, who is accustomed to phoning any of two or three colleagues around the town for advice and support and to beg copies of missing paperwork. 'Triad', indeed, started from just such an informal arrangement – the three heads are personal friends and had fallen into the habit of meeting occasionally in a pub to share ideas and problems.

The difference is that eighteen months ago Martin Tuck decided that it was time to make the arrangement more formal and to hold some meetings in school time – twice a term in the first instance. Then, as it became clear that a major feature of the meetings was the sharing of draft documents, the three bought fax machines and laptop computers with the same software.

Very quickly, though, they realized that they were often not able to cover promised ground, and were coming back together to find that deadlines had been missed. The answer was to employ freelance consultant Alan Craig.

A former employee of the authority, Alan Craig acts for fifty days a year as a professional assistant to 'Triad', minuting meetings and taking away draft documents for updating and circulation. (His considerable information technology and desktop publishing expertise is helpful here.) He also checks documents and policies against legal requirements.

The most tangible outcome so far from 'Triad' is that all three schools now have robust and well-documented policies in many of the major areas of curriculum and management.

One of the policies, in fact – that on Risk Assessment and Health and Safety – has generated considerable interest locally and is now marketed nationally by 'Triad Publications'. This is a clear pointer to future possibilities – there is work going on at the moment on a staff handbook and on a 'global planner' that brings together and charts every aspect of school life. (It sits on the computer and can be printed in various forms, including a big version for the staffroom wall.) The income generated from such projects is helping to offset the cost of buying Alan Craig's time.

Could other primary heads work in this way? 'Triad' members suggest that the critical factors are:

- A lively partnership based on existing professional friendship. Their view is that three is exactly the right number.
- The schools should be similar but not have adjoining catchment areas – any element of competition would introduce a wrong note.

At the same time, 'Triad' members are quick to disclaim any idea that they have found the complete answer to primary management. 'It works for us' is their common refrain. So, for example, although this group relies heavily on the skills of Alan Craig, another 'Triad' in another place would obviously develop its own way of working, using whichever outside skills were available or affordable. Alan Craig himself does not want 'to give the impression that whoever does this kind of job has to have my background'.

'Triad', though, makes a convincing case for the idea that there is a space to be filled somewhere between the informal get-together and the big consortium. It is, suggests Martin Tuck, 'a very positive way of staying sane through what are stressful and trying times!'

9

Primary consortia 2

The Ivel Schools' Association (ISA) in Bedfordshire is perhaps unusual in being, in effect, a cementing together of the 'pyramid' formed by a secondary school (Samuel Whitbread Upper) and eighteen of its associated nineteen middle and lower schools.

Another feature of the ISA is that governors are equal partners with heads at each level of organization. Chair of the Association, for example, is John Tizard, who is also Chair of Governors at Etonbury Middle, one of the member schools, and a governor at Samuel Whitbread. The Association's roots, he explained, go back to the post-general election days of 1992.

'There was a feeling that the government would continue the thrust towards making schools grant maintained. We'd always had good cross-phase co-operation in this area; we were very keen to keep that and to retain a relationship with the local authority.'

So, from a series of exploratory and planning meetings, the Association slowly emerged over the following year. There was support from the authority – an officer was assigned to help with administration – and governing bodies decided, one by one, to join, at a subscription which amounts to 0.4 per cent of each school's budget.

The Association was formally established in February 1994. Its stated aims included securing a greater level of budget delegation from the authority to member schools, promoting curriculum projects, promoting cross-phase continuity, mutual support for heads and 'The presentation of state schools on a non-competitive basis'.

Actual projects over the year have included joint management across the schools – with consequent significant savings – of the delegated budget for peripatetic music teachers. The Association also handled the combined budget for special needs training.

Interestingly, any idea that the Association might be a purchasing consortium – high on the agenda in some other groupings – has only a brief mention in the development plan, which continues to concentrate on curriculum initiatives, training, possible joint teacher appointments in the special needs area, and an expressed intention to work with authority staff on delegation. (The Association is helping the authority to pilot full delegation of the structural repairs and maintenance budget.) Paul Brett, Bedfordshire's Deputy CEO, feels that it is the focus on the curriculum which will in the end be of most interest to schools involved in consortia.

'There has to be a payback for schools, and I believe that they will benefit most if it's curricular – if the group helps schools to cope with change rather than being a financial, trading body.'

The relationship with the authority is crucial, and the ISA, in common with other similar groups, is at pains to develop it. Bedfordshire, for its part, explained Mr Brett, 'welcomes groups like this because they are handy local mechanisms by which we can communicate with schools – in a way it's like setting up a mini-area office. And they give schools the opportunity to address local authority services in the way that is most economic to them. It's yet another way of redefining the centre's relationship with its schools.'

The key to all consortia of this kind is how the central administration is to be handled – is the administrator a bursar/secretary, for example, or a higher level manager? 'We certainly wanted someone who would carry credibility with heads,' explained John Tizard, who was surprised at the level of interest shown by applicants, 'given that it was only a one-year appointment at £25,000'.

In the end, the post was filled by Dr Ron Wallace who has been a secondary head, Hertfordshire's Chief Adviser, and an independent OFSTED inspector. He pointed out that 'The title of co-ordinator is important. My only agenda is that of the nineteen schools.'

He has a modest office at Etonbury and is assisted by a secretary, but is at pains to emphasize that there is determination in the ISA to avoid setting up a bureaucracy which contains the seeds of growth. His advice is 'Not to set up anything permanent that can't be changed'. And suiting action to the words, he considerably reduced his working hours in the second year and increased the hours of the secretary, cutting administration costs overall by thirty per cent, from £50,000 in the first year to £35,000 in the second. 'I'm aware that every penny spent by schools on us is money the schools could have spent on other things.'

10

Admission plan

Secondary schools these days compete with each other for pupils. Each pupil brings funding to the school and it pays, therefore – quite literally – to leave nothing to chance during the time when parents are choosing schools. Rising pupil numbers mean more money, and therefore better staffing and better resources. Here Neville Beischer describes how his own school goes about making sure that it enrols all of its potential pupils.

A month-by-month admissions plan

With school budgets so heavily dependent on pupil numbers, a full intake each year is vital. A loss of even ten pupils from the predicted intake can mean a corresponding staff reduction of one-and-a-half teachers.

Increased parental choice has increased competition, especially in urban areas where several schools are often close together.

We are on the eastern side of Manchester and have some fifteen secondary schools within a two-and-a-half mile radius, many of which are competing for a share of the pupils who live locally.

Our neighbours include two of the top independent schools in the country, two single-sex ex-grammars (both grant maintained), three Catholic comprehensives and eight other comprehensives, including my own.

It would be nice to believe that Wright Robinson's good reputation would be enough to ensure a full intake each September. However, I realize that the drive by many of the schools around us to recruit pupils is gathering pace all the time. My school, the largest 11 to 16 in the city, has to fill more than 300 places each September – this cannot be left to chance.

Past experience has taught us how dangerous complacency can be. Four years ago our intake dropped from 300-plus to 180 with almost disastrous consequences. However, for the past three years we have been consistently over-subscribed, I believe as a result of a vigorous and comprehensive recruitment and marketing campaign. It involves simple and straightforward strategies.

September:

- Search for prospective pupils' names and addresses; our pupils are asked if they know of any Year 6 brother, sister, cousin, friend, etc., thinking of coming to us.
- Full check with partner primary schools for names and addresses of Year 6 pupils in their school.
- Build up a register of all possible Year 6 prospective pupils for entry next September.
- Our swimming pool rota is drawn up, allowing partner primary school pupils use during the day.
- Autumn term school newspaper professionally produced with the last summer's GCSE results.
- Coaching courses set up for local Year 6 pupils in major school sports.
- Photographs of Year 7 pupils taken while they work for use in next year's school literature and for new front entrance display.

October:

- Secondary school taster days organized for all Year 6 local primary school pupils.
- Current Year 7 pupils in school uniform accompanied by high school staff return to their former primary school to take part in assemblies.
- All possible Year 6 prospective pupils for entry next September are sent our 'starter pack' which includes school newspaper; school pen, pencil, rubber and ruler; invitation to open evening.
- Open evening organized: adverts placed in the local press; posters taken to all local primary schools for display; pupils also take posters for display in shops around the city.

November:

- High school brochure and information sent to partner primary schools for distribution to Year 6 parents, along with LEA secondary schools request form.
- High school brochures distributed to other local primaries and parents on request.
- Personal tours and interviews organized for prospective pupils and parents.

December:

- Welcome letters sent to all parents who have chosen our high school with uniform list.
- Personal tours and interviews for prospective parents and pupils continue.
- Personal follow-up by a senior member of staff on every enquiry.

January and February:

- Follow-up on parents who are still undecided on school choice. Close liaison with LEA on confirming numbers and names of pupils allocated places, and those on the waiting lists.
- Reassurance given to parents on the waiting list that they are not forgotten.

March:

- Year 5 and Year 6 local primary pupils invited to see the school show, free transport provided.
- New brochure designed for next academic year.
- Advertising campaign for previous year evaluated and new strategies for next year discussed.
- Advertising budget decided on.
- Next year's new intake numbers finalized.

April and May:

- New school marketing stock ordered.

June and July:

- Induction days for new Year 7 pupils.
- Induction evenings for new parents.
- Local primary and infant schools sports day.

It is important to realize that 'marketing' only really works when the product offered is of the highest quality, one which you feel proud to be associated with. So when we initiated our marketing and recruitment campaign it was not done in isolation; we also implemented a full school improvement programme.

And if you are going to make promises to parents about your school, you must be prepared to honour them.

Neville Beischer is head of Wright Robinson High School, Gorton, Manchester.

11
Girls' achievement

Although it is entirely right that senior staff appointments should be free of gender bias, it is also true that the heads and governors of mixed schools should continue to ensure that girls are not marginalized, and their particular needs overlooked. Here Kate Myers points out the need for mixed schools to be more 'girl-friendly'.

The publication of exam results raises once again the issue of girls' achievements; they are doing better than boys at SATs and at GCSE. Girls' schools often fare better in the league tables and mixed schools with a balanced intake of girls are likely to do better than schools with a predominantly male intake and all-boys' schools.

Many mixed schools near a single-sex girls' school have a preponderance of boys, partly because there are slightly more male pupils in the school population but also, and perhaps more importantly, because girls' schools in the state system continue to be more popular than boys'.

What can mixed schools do? It is unlawful to try to balance admission by sex, so they must try to attract more female pupils by becoming more 'girl-friendly'.

One starting point would be to find out what pupils think.

Recent research into pupils' perception and choice of secondary schools has revealed how influential their views are in the decision about which secondary school they attend. It also seems that male and female pupils are influenced by different factors about prospective schools.

Researchers who interviewed primary pupils before choices were made and after places had been allocated found that more boys than girls had picked schools which they thought had good science, sports, computing and practical facilities, whereas girls were more concerned about what was available for dance and music. Girls appeared to be generally less knowledgeable about the facilities in the school of their choice.

Both boys and girls chose schools that were 'easy to get to, had large buildings, and good opportunities for girls and boys'. Both sexes thought that being able to study areas of the curriculum traditionally associated with the other sex was a reason for choosing a mixed school. Although more Asian and Afro-Caribbean pupils chose single-sex schools, the majority opted for mixed. Boys of all ethnic groups were more worried about the prevalence of bullying, gangs and violence in secondary schools; girls were more concerned about the prevalence of smoking.

Being aware of the clients' interests and concerns should help schools develop appropriate marketing strategies. However, unless there are some fundamental changes, more dissatisfied clients may be produced who will, in turn, become wary customers when they are parents. I find it increasingly depressing to speak to groups of girls in different types of schools who, with unremitting frequency, make the same points about the quality of their schooling experience.

The most frequent (and invariably justified) complaint is about the state of the toilets. The list of concerns includes no soap, no toilet paper, no towels, no working sanitary incinerator, no tampons. Many schools sell these provisions from the school office without realizing what a potentially embarrassing scenario they are setting up for shy female pupils.

School toilets are sometimes locked and as menstruation does not always restrict itself to starting at break-or lunch-time, getting hold of the key can be an excruciating experience for a girl who has already had to extricate herself from a classroom, possibly being forced to explain to a male teacher why she cannot wait till break-time.

Younger girls are sometimes intimidated by the older 'regulars' who congregate in the toilets for warmth and often to smoke. Toilets suffer from vandalism – the reason often given to explain their state – but vandal-proof facilities can be installed as in most public conveniences. It is also possible to work with the girls to encourage them to feel some responsibility for the maintenance of decent facilities. Consideration could also be given to providing separate toilets for the younger pupils.

Other concerns include different curricular provision, particularly in PE. Not all the girls I spoke to want to do mixed PE and games, but most want the opportunity to play the same games, particularly football and rugby. Many also object to having to wear a different PE kit.

There is a strong feeling of injustice in the few remaining schools that still do not allow girls to wear trousers (probably against the Sex Discrimination Act), particularly amongst the older girls.

Another frequent complaint is about the playground being dominated by boys and that there is nowhere for girls to go at break- and lunch-times. (If this problem could be resolved it might reduce the numbers of 'regulars' in the toilets.)

Less frequently, but not uncommonly, I am told stories about 'no-go' areas in schools where boys congregate inappropriately to call names or even to touch female pupils passing by. I am still shocked when I hear black girls talk about name-calling and how many of them just resign themselves to it.

I have only met one girl who felt there was no one she could speak to on the staff if she had problems. Most girls speak highly of their teachers. Most do not describe themselves as unhappy at school, but by listening to and acting on what they tell us, we could make their experience a much happier one. These satisfied 'customers' will spread the word and the schools that try seriously to address these issues may find their imbalance of girls and boys is redressed. Their bonus could be that they will look better in future league tables.

Kate Myers is a senior inspector in a London borough.

12
Staff training

What is a training day for? Several studies have suggested that secondary teachers often feel that school training days do not, in fact, match their needs. But in a big school there are many needs, and what may be right for the school may not be a high priority for a department or an individual. Here, Martin Baxter discusses some of these dilemmas.

Some research suggests teachers feel there is too little connection between training and what happens in the classroom. And the problems seem to be worse in secondary schools. In a MORI poll of 7800 schools, completed for the Teacher Training Agency in 1995, almost a third of teachers did not regard all of their training days as having been used for training and several studies have suggested that secondary heads are losing touch with the training needs of their staff. Heads appear to give training days a higher priority than teachers who feel too much time is spent in meetings, looking at school-wide issues determined by senior management, instead of meeting subject needs.

In contrast, studies in primary schools show that headteachers and teachers have similar priorities. The smaller staff team and broader curriculum interests mean the needs of the school also determine those of individual members of staff. The daily debate in a primary school staffroom is more likely to include the headteacher who, as the leading professional, can shape opinion and ensure that all staff are involved in the organization and planning of training. Training days can then develop policies while expanding the staff's skills and knowledge.

In secondary schools, local management has tended to distance the head from educational leadership and teaching. Hierarchical management has been replaced by flatter structures and an emphasis on strategic planning, with increased responsibility and account-ability devolved to subject and pastoral teams. This means the relatively equal status among teachers in primary schools is applied to ten or a dozen teams in secondary schools and is a recipe for anarchy and discontinuity of learning unless the school's priorities are very clear.

Businesses are learning that there is a balance between short-term business strategy – their equivalent of improving the teaching of a specific topic – in separate departments and planning for change and long-term success in the whole business. Organizations such as Shell have been able to respond to rapid change because senior managers have been removed from fire-fighting so they can think about the longer term. Is a large school with 100 staff and 1000 pupils so different?

It is not surprising that a hard-pressed teacher who desperately needs to revise a work scheme reacts negatively to a training day devoted to team-building or liaison with primary schools. The headteacher, on the other hand, might think that such a day chal-lenged perceptions, made a statement about school priorities and laid the foundation for subsequent work at department level.

The TTA is rightly concerned that many schools do not yet have a systematic approach to professional development or an understand-ing of how in-service budgets actually affect what happens in class-rooms. This is an issue that local authorities and the government have failed to solve.

Commercial organizations are responding to the challenge of pro-viding a product or service that meets customers' needs in the short term, while planning for long-term success, by motivating those people within the organizations who can provide a high-quality service or are capable of rapid innovation.

When this professional development is translated to schools, it is likely to include:

- focusing on the future;
- preparing the medium-term plan;
- achieving short-term objectives within a department;
- transforming individuals;
- transforming the school.

Achieving short-term goals within a department is very important but there are other, less obvious priorities. Responding to requests from the School Development Plan team can easily be another chore to be ignored. Yet, increasingly it informs governors about the implementation of policies, determines whole-school priorities for the next year, and identifies what is required at department level.

Department priorities can improve the competence of all staff, and fast tracking and special projects provide new ways of using talent and expertise. An important role for the headteacher and senior managers is to think about the future and ensure that knowledge, skills and processes are being developed to meet the changing needs of pupils and the curriculum.

Training days are a valuable resource. However, staff costs alone for a large secondary school could be in excess of £6,000 a day, so perhaps evaluating whether training days provide value for money could be a priority. It may not always be obvious to the participants what the long-term intentions are. But when the objectives allow a department team to shape its own destiny, the benefits can be rapid.

A training day may be concerned with preparing for a switch in emphasis next year, challenging accepted norms, or laying the foundations for an anticipated change, the details of which are still unclear. None of these are likely to impact immediately on teaching and learning, and some teachers will certainly feel that their time on a training day has not been well used. However, in terms of developing the school as an organization, they are important issues to be discussed by the whole staff.

Checklist

- Were the outcomes of your last training day clear?
- What was the balance between individual, department and whole-school issues?
- Is the link between the school development plan and in-service training clear?
- Who does the long-term planning in your school?

Martin Baxter is professional tutor at Campion School, Bugbrooke, Northampton, responsible for development planning, staff induction and school-based teacher training.

13

Cross-phase liaison

Many heads and teachers believe that the move from primary to secondary school causes an interruption in the progress of pupils. The way to minimize this is to set up good liaison between the two sectors. This, though, can be easier said than done, when schools are deeply involved with internal priorities. Here, Gerald Haigh looks at a school which has tried to address the issue.

Kennet School – cross-phase liaison

So many things can go wrong when pupils move from primary to secondary school – individual needs missed, prior learning unrecognized, yawning gaps made apparent. Consequently, on both sides of the divide, stereotyped assumptions and hasty judgements start to breed – that primary children have inadequate specialist teaching; that secondary classroom practice is short on encouragement and warmth and long on confrontation and negative reinforcement.

One secondary head who recognizes both the importance and the difficulties of cross-phase liaison is Paul Dick, head of Kennet School in Berkshire. Mr Dick, a Member of SCAA, ran in 1995 an important cross-phase conference for neighbouring schools.

Although he was happy to run the conference, Paul Dick believes that the drive should really be coming from a higher level. 'I am continually dismayed that nobody central has said they are going to do anything significant about continuity. There is some work going on in SCAA, but nothing has been published yet. Neither does OFSTED show much interest, and I think that's regrettable. It's an area where there is tension on the ground, and yet no prompt coming from above. And this is one of the areas where there is potential for significant improvement.'

In fact, he pointed out, the growth of parental choice and competition for pupils is making things worse.

'The idea of one school feeding another has disappeared. Now you have primary heads wanting to be careful not to cause offence or difficulty for their secondary schools.'

And, of course, he suggested, teachers have had a lot of other things to do lately: 'Implementing the National Curriculum has put a lot of pressure on schools, and caused them to look inward and concentrate on the changes within.'

Nevertheless, since their conference, each of the departments at Kennet has had a fresh look at cross-phase curriculum continuity, under the overall direction of curriculum deputy head Sue Croft, who told me that 'We can't any longer say we'll start the new intake off again from the beginning, as if it doesn't matter what they've done before – which is exactly what many good teachers have done for so long.'

That task itself, though, has not been uniformly easy. 'There is concern in some areas at the lack of specialist knowledge and expertise at Key Stage 2.'

Nevertheless, Sue Croft described a range of departmental cross-phase initiatives, of which these are just some examples:

- Technology teachers in both phases have formed a group called 'Technology Teachers Together' which meets regularly to discuss curriculum issues and classroom practice.
- The Physical Education department is conducting an audit among partner primary schools to determine exactly what their pupils are covering.
- The Art department is running master classes for able junior school pupils, in techniques such as screen printing that they may not otherwise meet in Key Stage 2.
- A music teacher spends a double period a week teaching in primary schools.
- The local RE teachers' support group, formed for and by secondary specialists, has been opened up to primary teachers, and Kennet has passed on a number of artefacts and resources to primary schools.
- In humanities there are combined primary/secondary study topics – work on the history of the local church, for example.

- Primary classes visit the science department, and Kennet staff spend time co-operating with primary school planning and practice.

One very promising way forward, though, is for primary and secondary staff to work together on their understanding of National Curriculum levels. Ian Parsons, head of English at Kennet, explained that 'We're establishing a common portfolio of work. It was driven originally by concern about discrepancy in assessment.'

Much the same is happening in mathematics – a subject which in many schools is a focus of doubt about the accuracy of Key Stage 2 assessment. Kennet teachers have worked with primary colleagues not only on common understanding of levels, but also on what counts as proper mathematical content in investigative work ('Using and Applying Mathematics' in the National Curriculum). According to head of department Bev Pinsent, 'The different attitudes to investigation between subject-trained teachers and non-specialists was interesting, and we had a lot of debate about this kind of work.'

At Parsons Down Junior, which sends many of its children to Kennet, deputy head Dave Clarke agreed on the importance of teachers trusting each other on assessment. 'If the secondary school becomes confident and happy with our levels then that's a step forward. It's going to take time, though.'

What is clearly most important to Dave Clarke, however, is the underlying attitude. 'We don't feel that education stops at the end of Key Stage 2, and we hope that they no longer feel that education starts at Key Stage 3.'

He appreciates the efforts being made by the various Kennet departments to reach out to primary schools. 'Technology, particularly, has taken a big step forward.' He is convinced that the push from Kennet is in the best interests of the pupils. 'It's a very honest thing they are doing. There's no hidden agenda. For our part we do feel the need not to be wasting children's time in the secondary school – that's where teachers would give up many hours to be sure it's right.'

There is plenty still to be done – on, for example, the vexed question of what recorded information to pass on between phases. Here Kennet is doing interesting work on presenting pupil information graphically so that busy classroom teachers can take it in quickly without having to study tables of figures.

The teachers at Kennet and its partner primaries are certainly not claiming to have found all the answers to primary–secondary curriculum liaison. They have, though, identified some of the right questions, and are making time to address them. As Dave Clarke put it, 'It's a start. We've created an awareness of the problems, and hopefully we can keep going forward.'

14

The primary co-ordinator

In most primary schools every teacher except the head has a full-time teaching commitment – and in many small schools this goes for the head too. How, therefore, does the teacher in charge of a subject – a 'Subject Co-ordinator' – find time to do a job which assumes knowledge of what goes on in other classrooms, and also requires time for training and meetings? Here, Gerald Haigh looks at this highly intractable problem.

By contrast with that of the secondary head of department, the primary co-ordinator's position seems ill-defined – there is rarely a physically defined 'empire' of rooms and resources, for example, nor the opportunity to recruit and lead a team of fellow specialists. The very word 'co-ordinator', indeed, seems to have been deliberately chosen for its slightly vague, non-authoritarian associations. A co-ordinator, presumably, does not baldly tell people what to do (perish the thought) but works alongside fellow professionals so that they can develop their subject work together. Implicit in this arrangement is that the co-ordinator has specialist knowledge which will be brought tactfully into play, preferably on request.

It is not, obviously, an easy job, this subject-centred management responsibility in a child-centred collaborative environment. Not least of the difficulties is finding the time to do it. The vast majority of primary teachers have full-time class responsibility, so that the co-ordinator has limited opportunities for observing work in progress or for holding meetings in school hours. And, of course, every teacher in the average staffroom – often including the NQT – will be a co-ordinator, so that it is possible to see a modern primary school as a

Gilbertian place in which everyone is co-ordinating everybody else.

Despite the obvious problems, though, co-ordinators have shot into prominence in recent years. 'They are rising stars,' is how Essex infant head Louisa Sliwa put it when I discussed the issues with her. 'They have a really important role, especially in the core subjects.'

They have not, though, as Fred Corbett, Principal Adviser for School Development in Essex pointed out, risen from nowhere. 'There have been subject responsibilities right from the time of Bullock and Cockroft.' Any recent renewal of interest, he suggested, 'is partly because of OFSTED and the resurgence of the notion of monitoring and evaluation'.

Conventional wisdom is that the teaching profession has always been better at having ideas than at judging their effect, and Fred Corbett's mention of monitoring and evaluation puts a finger on what is potentially both the most important and the trickiest part of the co-ordinator's job. It is relatively easy for a keen co-ordinator to gather people around and say, 'This term, let's do these ten amazing things', and considerably more difficult to keep tabs on how well they are being done, and to tackle colleagues who are dragging their feet.

As Louisa Sliwa's account of managing the work of her own co-ordinators shows, the support of the head in all this is vital. 'Co-ordinators monitor their curriculum areas, going round each class, focusing on particular things and observing the teachers at work. From that they pick up training needs, and they may quietly go and work with a person who is finding an area difficult.'

Crucially, though, 'This is all reported back to me, and we have devised a pro forma for keeping notes on what needs to be done.'

Fred Corbett, too, mentioned the importance of writing things down. 'We've been saying that co-ordinators need to pick up on the notion of writing an annual report on their subject in the school – saying, what do I think about standards in the school now. We've explored the idea of attaching some of these to the head's report to governors.'

It is also the head's job, of course, to ensure that the co-ordinator has time for all of this, and there is increasing realization that subjects have to be picked up one or two at a time, in accordance with a programme set out in the School Development Plan. As Louisa Sliwa put it, 'You have to prioritize, or the thing becomes unmanageable and you're tinkering. If you want to implement change you have to do it in depth and detail.'

This implies that co-ordinators will wax and wane in prominence as time goes by, but that each in turn will attract investment of time and resources. 'I do try to give them time out if they are monitoring,' said Louisa Sliwa. 'I might say you can have Friday off to do that – it's not enough, but it's a token.'

Running through this notion of a rolling programme of development is the question of how far the school sees some subjects – and therefore some co-ordinators – as more important than others. Fred Corbett is wary of any policy which, in his words, 'reinforces a hierarchical view of the curriculum'. If, for example, a school supports core subjects over foundation subjects, with more resources and better paid co-ordinators, then it is at least arguable that it is not only introducing extra layers of hierarchy but is also working against the twin concepts of breadth and balance.

There are many uncertainties here, and much to discuss – something which is reflected in the amount of time and energy which local authorities and other trainers are putting into the support of primary co-ordinators. There is a real need for practical help of a kind which will help teachers actually to do the co-ordinating job at a time when class sizes are rising, budgets are being squeezed and non-contact time is increasingly a product of the creative use of whole-school hymn practices.

Part Two
Managing People

15

Women in senior management

The task of the modern secondary deputy is complicated by some of the historical baggage that the job carries. For example, it was taken for granted for many years that in mixed secondary schools there should be a 'Senior Mistress' – perhaps with deputy head status – who would have special responsibility for 'girls' welfare'. Only gradually did the assumptions underlying this division of responsibility begin to be challenged. Even now, although the wording of job descriptions and vacancy advertisements are strictly controlled, the underlying reality may well hark back to an earlier time, as Rosemary Litawski found when she looked into the reality behind the rhetoric.

It is part of the folklore of teaching that some deputy posts are intended for women, others for men. The Sex Discrimination Act makes clear it is unlawful to imply that applicants from one sex will not be considered. To advertise a deputy head's post with responsibility for 'girls' welfare' may imply that applications from men will not be considered. It disadvantages men, but it also disadvantages women.

The female deputy is often associated with a narrow range of tasks, characterized by a lower 'social–emotional' role as opposed to the more powerful 'task-instrumental' one.

It is a role more likely to be labelled 'pastoral' than 'academic', and portrays women as supportive, subordinate, maternal and caring a role that is often described in terms such as 'tea-dispenser', the 'Tampax and aspirin merchant', flower arranger, minute taker, or the 'nappies and noses touch'. It is a readily recognizable sexist role, which is sometimes embodied in the formal job description, with 'responsibility for girls' welfare', or is apparent in the more informal aspects of the role.

The title 'Senior Mistress and/or Second Mistress' had become an anachronism even before it disappeared with the 1988 conditions of employment, but it is a label that carried a powerful legacy of expectations of role, often obscured by familiarity. Yet the traditions of Senior Mistress and differentiation by gender at management level is so entrenched in some schools that it could be described as 'institutional sexism'. It is so taken for granted that its familiarity obscures its very existence. The legacy of expectation and one's predecessor's role has a tremendous influence on the present deputy. The title Senior Mistress may have disappeared; the role has not.

Over a six-month period from 2 December 1988 to 31 May 1989, I wrote off for the details of 378 job advertisements appearing in *The TES* for deputy headships of co-educational, maintained comprehensives.

Twelve specifically asked for responsibility for 'girls' welfare' and two for 'boys' welfare'. A further twelve job descriptions also listed 'girls' welfare' and, after analysis, a further sixty-four described a sex-stereotypical role. This was further substantiated by the fact that all the eighty-eight sex-stereotyped job descriptions named the previous incumbent as a woman.

The tasks and responsibilities required of the female deputy head were people-orientated and pastoral but, more revealingly, low-level operational tasks. Some were so demeaning as to be insulting, and certainly did not justify the salaries.

One post asked for someone 'to set a good example to staff and pupils in behaviour, dress and practice'. Another listed ten responsibilities, from 'probationary teachers, to annual charity drives, secondhand uniform and front-of-house at school plays and concerts'.

Others listed responsibility for school photographs, visitors, arrangements for school trips, allocation of locker keys, bus passes, wet weather routines, school bells, prize-giving arrangements, medical provision, minute taking, refreshments, and even . . . checking the skirting boards, toilets and curtains!

The most frequent tasks asked of women are: pastoral responsibilities; in-service training, grants for educational support and training and staff development; links with external agencies, especially education welfare agencies; records of achievements; staff substitution and supply teachers; girls' welfare and probationers and students. And a new task emerging on some job descriptions – responsibility for 'equal opportunities'.

National statistics indicate that about one-third of all secondary head deputies are female. Consequently, it is possible to suggest and anticipate that for the 378 advertised posts, women will be appointed to 126 of them. If eighty-eight job descriptions described a sex-stereotypical role, then about seventy per cent of the posts for deputy headships for women are expecting a sex-stereotypical, low-status role. This must be an immediate cause for concern.

But advertisements and job descriptions can be different from reality, and things may change once someone is in post.

During the summer term of 1990, I contacted all seventeen secondary schools listed on one page of the education authority directory. Thirty-five of the forty-one deputy heads returned a questionnaire, and I interviewed thirty-nine. Of the thirteen female deputy heads I interviewed, over half had responsibility for tasks that were predominantly pastoral, social and emotional, and which had lower status than those of their male colleagues. Only two were responsible for the timetable, and only one for finance.

One described 'having been trapped into doing the "cover" for the past eight years' and envisaging doing it till she retired. Another described her role as 'girls' problems, girls' discipline, first aid, the key register ... it's an absolute killer of a job, and, of course, I am third deputy'.

Several described intense feelings of loneliness, marginalization, isolation, alienation, frustration and anger, in varying degrees, at their lack of strategic role. One had resigned after being in post only two terms.

A key factor influencing the female deputy's present role was the wording of the original advertisement and, subsequently, the head's and the staff's expectations, often based on the predecessor's role. Interviews with both male and female deputies revealed that the relationship with the head was a prime factor in determining and negotiating deputies' roles. Stereotypical expectations by a head could result in any range of tasks being low status and operational.

Revealingly, only one of the thirteen female deputies was currently making applications for headship. None could be described as oozing confidence and ambition. None had a career plan, in contrast to more than one-third of the male deputies.

In March 1991, one advertisement in *The TES* for a deputy head wanted someone with responsibility for 'girls' welfare'. It was in an LEA school with an equal opportunities policy. I was given permission to observe the selection and appointment of the deputy head, and to study her role to the end of her first year in post.

During the interviewing of the four female candidates, I heard discriminatory questions and, as anticipated, saw a woman appointed to the sex-stereotyped post. The head claimed it was an act of positive discrimination in order to attract a female to the senior management team. The LEA officer never questioned the sexist role, and yet the senior inspector (female) in the authority had replied to my initial exploratory letter asking for her support, that she 'viewed the research as unnecessary and provocative'.

Denial of the problem appears to be increasing. Sex-stereotypical roles are assumed to be an issue of the past, associated with the days of the appointment of a senior mistress. The Secondary Heads Association's latest study of deputy heads last year feels gender to be so insignificant that it was not considered as a variable.

However, by the end of her first year in post, the female deputy had assumed a pastoral, people-person role, whereas her male colleague was responsible for the timetable, curriculum and finance. Promotion would be difficult without the experience of finance.

Despite being a forceful personality and an ambitious individual, she was in a role in many ways moulded by her predecessor and the advertisement.

It has been suggested that the 'new market-economy' approach in education, and the increased importance of financial matters, could lead not only to the increased specialization of roles, but also the reappearance of traditional deputy roles. S. Darlington (*TES*, 12 June 1992) argues that women will suffer further discrimination with the new macho management style of schools. 'Governors will be more biased towards men because of the increased responsibilities in finance.'

Could grant-maintained status and schools taking more responsibility for their own budgets mean more male heads?

Department for Education figures show that the number of women being appointed to secondary headships today is even lower than three years ago. Less than one per cent of women teachers are secondary heads. A sex-stereotypical role cannot prepare women for headship.

Rosemary Litawksi is a secondary head.

16

Equal opportunity

The article by Rosemary Litawski clearly challenges heads and governors to be fair and equitable in their recruitment practices.

John Green has done research into secondary school recruitment and found that schools were quite commonly doing things that could bring them into conflict with equal opportunity legislation. Here are some guidelines that should help.

My research into recruitment, selection and equal opportunities in eleven secondary schools found common practices which leave those responsible for appointments open to allegations of illegal discrimination.

When a school has a vacancy, it is normally essential to compile a job description containing such information as its title, location, pay, who the post holder is accountable to – and for whom the person is responsible. It will also contain a list of responsibilities.

Some heads framed the job description for a man or for a woman. This is, of course, potentially illegal unless the job qualifies as an exception under the Sex Discrimination Act 1975. Section 7 (2) (e) defines an exception when 'the holder of the job provides individuals with personal services promoting their welfare or education, or similar personal services, and those services can most effectively be provided by a (man or woman)'. The advertisement for such a job would contain the statement: 'This advertisement is placed under Section 7 (2) (e) of the Sex Discrimination Act 1975 and exemption from the general provisions is claimed.' Complaints can still be made when the advertisement appears, but this has not happened often.

Next is the preparation of the person specification, which defines the skills, qualifications, experience and personal qualities required for the job. These requirements may be divided into those that are essential and those that are simply desirable. Again, it is possible to be illegally discriminatory. Words or phrases can be included which favour men or women or disadvantage people from the ethnic minorities.

In my survey, two heads were not aware of the legal requirement to ensure equal opportunities in the preparation of these documents. Read them carefully three times: first as a woman would read it; second, from a man's point of view; and third as if one were from the ethnic minorities.

The advertisement is generally based on the contents of the job description and the person specification. Advertisements should contain filters to prevent an avalanche of unsuitable applications. The ideal is, perhaps, 15–25 applications from which to compile a short list – another hazardous process. One head told me that she tries to arrive at a male/female/ethnic minority balance for her short list. Such positive discrimination is also potentially illegal.

The correct procedure should be to compare each application with the job description and essentials of the person specification. If there are too many applicants to interview, bring in the 'desirable' column of the person specification. CVs are only likely to tell you what the applicant wants you to know.

If a multitude of applications is received, it is not illegal to 'draw out of a hat' a number of, say, six or eight to interview. However, be sure to put all applications in the 'draw', without exception.

Research suggests experienced interviewers do not make more reliable decisions than inexperienced ones. In fifteen-minute interviews, the decision is often made in the first four minutes. Negative information from a candidate carries more weight than positive; structured interviews are more reliable than unstructured.

Managers often admit to being 'turned off' by bald men, ginger hair, beards, men wearing earrings or inappropriate dress. Some might add to this list black and disabled people. Aspects of candidates that 'turned interviewers on' included appropriate dress, eye contact, smiles at appropriate times, a conventional hairstyle and motivation towards the job rather than the money.

In my research, many schools took into account such things as the candidates' 'behaviour' during a school walkabout or over lunch. This can only be subjective decision making and should not form a part of the selection process.

In a structured interview, the panel should ask each candidate the same carefully pre-planned questions with supplementaries for clarification. Each interviewer should have criteria in mind for the ideal answer and should assess the extent to which the candidate meets those criteria. The questions should be weighted from the most important to the least by the panel and each candidate's response marked against the weighted number.

This will not magically produce a successful candidate, but it will give a basis for discussion. Weak areas may be quickly spotted, as may the extent to which candidates have met the job description and person specification. These are your criteria: you should not compare one candidate with another.

Asking questions at interview is the most difficult area. If questions about marital status, number of children, domestic circumstances, views of partners on applications, starting a family, caring for dependants, partner moving jobs or candidate's ethnic origin are asked at interview or used as a key factor in rejecting someone at decision-making time, there is a serious risk of an allegation of sex or race discrimination. An industrial tribunal will almost certainly demand to see all of the papers relating to the vacancy as well as hear evidence from each member of the interview panel. There is now no limit to the financial award against a school if found guilty of unlawful discrimination.

John Green is a senior lecturer and was formerly a personnel manager in the public sector.

17

The primary deputy

The role of the deputy is being reviewed also in the primary sector, in line with the changing nature of the head's task. The following article by Gerald Haigh looks at research into the work of the primary deputy. He suggests that deputies need to convince their paymasters of the uniqueness and importance of what they do.

Are you a primary deputy? Then let me play the role of a hard boiled, cost-conscious governor and ask why on earth you think we need you.

'There are, after all, only two sorts of teachers in our school. On the one hand there is the head, who has an office, telephones, a computer workstation, a secretary and a light teaching load. And on the other there are our faithful classroom teachers who surface from their all-consuming task only at break, lunch-time and during hymn practice. How is it possible for one of these classroom teachers to contribute more significantly than any of the others to either the strategic management of the school or its day-to-day administration? Are we not paying a lot of extra money to someone whose extra work consists of a ragbag of low-level responsibilities such as taking Wednesday assembly, running the annual sports day and dealing with difficult parents when the head is away on a course?

'It seems to me that you are a luxury we could do without. Even were we to compensate by paying two or three of the other teachers a small administration allowance, we would still save money. And, I might say, this would be entirely in line with what is happening in my own firm, where the fashion for "flattening the hierarchy" aka "de-layering", seems likely to threaten my own position.'

I suggest that having read this, primary deputy, you now have one of three sets of feelings.

Perhaps you feel a bit guilty. You have thirty-five children in your class, and little or no contact time. You are maths co-ordinator, and this alone takes up more time than you have available. You teach in the leaky hut across the playground – an act of self-sacrifice on your part – and you hardly see the head during the day. The head is energetic and effective, and clearly wants to get on with things rather than wait until you have a moment to talk. Every day, you suffer a little pang of self-reproach when you remember that you are being paid for a job which seems impossible. If it were not for the mortgage, you would ask to step down. Certainly you would sleep better at night.

Or perhaps you are hopping mad. You earn every penny of your allowance. You and the head work in partnership. You have clear areas of responsibility and leadership, and the governors spend money on relieving you from class to do your job.

Or possibly you are very frustrated. You thirst to share the tasks of management. You are busy, but you would find the time. The staff look up to you, and you know you could add significantly to the quality of their professional lives were you given access to decision making. The head, though, is always telling you that you have more than enough to do, every day while taking home paperwork that you could help with.

Whatever the fairness of the opening argument, it seems inevitable that, as class sizes increase, and non-contact time becomes more difficult to finance, it will become increasingly difficult for the primary deputy to have a job which matches the title.

The problem has been examined by a number of researchers, and is reviewed in detail in an article by Rosemary Webb and Graham Vulliamy of York University who found that: 'As the demands made on deputies continue to expand, the time available to meet these demands is contracting.'

The picture they report is of deputies who not only find it difficult to keep up the exemplary quality of their own teaching, but are losing touch with such management functions as budgeting and working with governors.

The challenge, then, is to define the primary deputy's role and justify it in terms of its cost. It means, for example, that it is not enough to see a deputy head merely as someone who is on the way to headship. For one thing, governors are not primarily in business to train heads for other people, and for another, there are now lots of deputies who do not want headship and whose need is for the job to be rewarding on its own terms.

One way forward is for heads and deputies to come to a job-sharing agreement – to write down both job descriptions and then decide who will do what.

The most important ingredient in the effectiveness of the partner-ship is the attitude of the head. This being so, it helps to know that there is already plenty of evidence to show that adding the deputy's strengths to those of the head increases the effectiveness of the school. In their book *School Matters*, a study of good London pri-mary schools published in 1988 (Open Books), Peter Mortimore and his fellow authors found that pupils reaped direct benefit in schools where the head involved the deputy in decision making. Pointing out the significance of this in *Managing Schools Today* in December 1995 ('Two Heads are Better than One'), Geoff Southworth of the University of Cambridge Institute of Education wrote that 'The role of the deputy is . . . not confined to administration, it is also deeply implicated in the children's attainment and progress.' Developing this theme, in the same article, Dr Southworth suggested that the deputy should become an 'Assistant Head', 'fully involved in the management, leadership and development of the school'.

The importance of partnership is being underlined by the work which Geoff Southworth did with advisers and deputy heads in Hertfordshire, where there is a well-established county-wide support network for primary deputies. As one aspect of this, a small group of primary deputies looked closely at those head/deputy partnerships which were identified by the authority as successful, and interviewed the partners with the aim of finding out what makes the chemistry work. Reporting the findings, in articles in *Primary School Manage-ment* and in *School Management Today*, Geoff Southworth identified a range of characteristics which are commonly identified by heads and deputies in successful partnerships. These include such qualities as a shared philosophy, mutual professional respect, a high degree of trust and – mentioned particularly – good communication, both formal and informal.

All of this, however, begs a number of questions, of which the most obvious is to do with how the deputy head, who is almost always a class teacher, is going to find the time to do the job. Signifi-cantly, heads in the successful Hertfordshire partnerships all acknowledged the importance of giving their deputies non-contact time. One head is reported as saying, 'I would fight tooth and nail to protect the non-contact time even if it meant the rest of the staff had to lose out.'

Deputies interviewed by me confirmed that time management is a recurring issue. One told me that 'The opportunity to have a block of quality time seems to make a real difference.' Another deputy pointed to her own example. 'My head negotiated my 0.1 (nought point one) non-contact time directly with the governors.'

(The point was made, though, that the limits to non-contact time in the primary school are not just financial. Class teachers, especially of younger children, are often reluctant to hand too much time over to supply teachers.)

Governors may want to know, suggested Geoff Southworth, that the non-contact time is being productively used. 'Time is a precious resource. Is it simply being used to make the deputy's life more tolerable?'

Deputies take this point, but believe that, in fact, time these days is used for specific purposes – recording and assessment was mentioned, and it was suggested that 'One that's coming more to the fore is evaluation and monitoring.'

The reluctance of heads to delegate does remain an obstacle to the development of true partnership. This reluctance often stems from well-meaning motives – in one authority, appraisal of heads shows them to be wary of delegating more for fear of overloading already busy deputies.

The danger here, though, suggested Geoff Southworth, is of being unclear about what delegation involves. 'It's necessary to distinguish between simply giving the deputy more jobs to do on the one hand and involving them fully in management on the other.'

Deputies, he believes, do want to be involved and to know what is happening. 'They have a great thirst for information.'

But if so much hangs on the head, does this leave the frustrated deputy with nothing to do other than go home and kick the cat? This seems to be where the support group comes in. The experience is that such a group acts as personal support, helps the exchange of information and is a vehicle for professional development. Importantly, too, it considerably raises the profile of primary deputy headship within the authority, bringing concerns into view and making heads collectively aware of the aspirations and needs of their deputies. Any group of determined deputies, it seems, could start a self-help network, but it is clear that the backing of the authority makes the enterprise much more effective and influential.

In the end, how a governing body sees the deputy when the budget starts to bite will depend very much on what they and the head think of the present incumbent. Importantly, therefore, the primary head needs to carve out a job which is positive and well defined.

Checklist for the primary deputy

- Seek a genuine management role – make a list, with the head, of management responsibilities, and decide which ones you can do.
- Then ask for time – half a day a week is not unreasonable in an average primary school.
- Ask to attend at least some governors, meetings.
- Ask to be involved in, or at least to observe, financial and budgeting procedures.
- Lead some staff meetings.
- Join up with other deputies – informally at first, perhaps later more formally in a support group. When this is starting to take shape, seek support from the authority.

18

Industrial placement

As heads begin to believe that there are generic issues which are common across businesses and schools, they also begin to see the point of industrial placement. In any case, it seems sensible to assume that it does heads and teachers good to let them see working life outside school.

Often, though, it goes no further than that – the teacher has an enjoyable experience, but it all soon wears off and nobody is really sure what it was all for. If industrial placement is to have a lasting effect, some planning has to be done. This article by Gerald Haigh is based on a secondary head's view of how industrial placement should be handled for the best effect.

Putting purpose into industrial placements

A primary head known to me once spent two weeks working in a butchers' shop, cutting up stewing steak, making pies and trying to find ten minutes in an eleven-hour day for a cup of tea. I also know an infant head who spent two weeks with a transport firm, going on the lorries as well as studying the office systems. The issue of which drivers were allowed the privilege of taking her on the road caused, I am told, seismic and far-reaching ructions throughout the organization.

Industrial placements of all kinds are increasingly common. Mention them approvingly in a meeting and everyone enthusiastically nods, because there has always been a general feeling that somehow they are a good thing for everyone. To what extent, though, do schools take advantages of the benefits? How far do any lessons which are learned spread beyond the people directly involved?

It was questions like these that exercised Tamsyn Imison, head of

Hampstead School, when she reflected on her own placement in 1995 with the North West Thames Regional Health Authority. In a report on industrial placements prepared for the Open University she wrote: 'I found that six months on, I had still done very little to make sure that my experience was shared . . . Even more alarming to me, as Head, was finding that of the other 22 members of staff who had been out on industry placements, only three reports had been written and that these were tucked away in a filing cabinet.'

Deciding to look further into this, Tamsyn Imison found a wealth of evidence to support the view that lack of planning was preventing the full benefits of placements from being realized. She quoted Prue Huddleston, of Warwick University's Centre for Education and Industry, for example: 'The greatest single failing was that in very few cases had the placements grown out of the general objectives set for the school.' Further confirmation came from Tamsyn Imison's own programme of interviews with colleagues involved in industrial placements in other schools, from which she drew up a list of the factors which are seen as important for making the most of placements. In order of importance these were:

- A positive senior management team.
- Structured policy linked to SDP and professional development planning.
- Teams with joint planning.
- Accredited link with Higher Education.
- A formal Industry Link.
- Use of UBI (Understanding British Industry) or similar agency.
- Use of External Audit.

Tamsyn Imison tried hard to sell to schools the idea of putting their industrial placement programme into the context of whole-school development. Taking advantage of her membership of the Council of the Secondary Heads Association, she produced for SHA a flier to all members which asked 'Do you get the most from your teacher placements in industry?' and which incorporated both the above list of significant factors and a list of aims based on those she produced for Hampstead School.

'Unless you link your teacher placements with a proper policy it's likely to be a waste of money. You really need to get it formally organized before you start because people go out with all the goodwill in the world – they have costly training and experience which actually doesn't bring in benefit.'

The danger then, is that 'with tight budgets it's likely to disappear altogether. An awful lot of staff don't realize the cost of cover, for example. It's a massive investment.'

Driven by the desire to put her thoughts and experiences into action, Tamsyn Imison revised procedures at Hampstead School to support her commitment to industrial placements. 'Obviously if we're putting the investment in we expect a clear bonus for the school – it's the sort of thing that OFSTED are looking at after all.' Hampstead School's Aims Statement on Teacher Placements summarizes the school's current approach:

1 To support the school's aims by linking closely with the targets set out in the Institutional Development Plan.
2 To support school teams in furtherance of their IDP targets.
3 To further teachers' professional development targets as agreed by appraisal.
4 To enlarge and enhance a teacher's professional experience.
5 To develop an understanding of the nature and change in the world of work.
6 To enhance the curriculum and the management of the school.
7 To enhance business contacts of value to the school.
8 To gain access to resources of value to the school.
9 To develop and update teachers' skills of use in the classroom:
10 To update information, advice and support for student career decisions.
11 To increase work experience placements for students.

Placements are subject to financial constraints and must be agreed within the INSET and Professional Development Budgets.

19

Performance-related pay

Schools constantly point out that by far their biggest running cost is the teachers' salary bill. One response to this is to suggest that the money should be more efficiently used – directed, perhaps, towards the people who are doing the best work.

Relating pay to performance, after all, seems like common sense – the better you do, the more money you earn. It is an equation which continues to attract, in particular, politicians whose responsibility is to see that limited resources are wisely used. However, as Bruce Douglas points out here, the reality of putting performance-related pay (PRP) into action is something else.

The first myth about performance-related pay is that the whole of the outside world has it and education cannot continue to live in an ivory tower. In fact, almost nobody is really paid by results. Most quoted examples are overwhelmingly one of two kinds of fake, in which:

- part of the pay is called 'performance bonus', but everybody receives it except the one in 100 who can't reach first base;
- some nominated 'output' figure reached or exceeded by a certain amount results in extra payment according to a formula (a chief executive receives ten per cent extra for each ten per cent increase in profit, or a football league manager receives £20,000 for ending the season as one of the top six teams or £100,000 for winning the championship).

The first of these has no real relationship to results and no significant motivating effect. It is a penalty for the abysmal. The second is much rarer and looks like genuine PRP, but there is no real connection between the achievement of the target figures and the reward for the recipients. If all football managers are trying equally hard to win the league, directors relying on PRP to motivate have no edge.

There is usually no evidence that where businesses offering PRP do achieve results, PRP is the cause. Where the bosses get paid for results, there is no greater success rate than where they just get paid. Usually these schemes are simply ways of paying high fees to attracts particular individuals.

The second myth about PRP is that teachers are *not* paid for their performance already. This is untrue. The monthly salary is paid for monthly work done and of course teaching is one of the 'performing arts' *par excellence*, second only to the theatre, and like it in that if you lose the audience life is hell. The performance pay currently being touted suggests something else – payment by specific indicators. Often, people who advocate PRP have in mind an unproved theory about how to lever up performance by pretending that some of these indicators are caused directly by named people and can reliably be taken as evidence of education of the kind we want.

Neither pretence is true. Nor is PRP necessary for goal-setting if that is wanted. Management by objectives is forty years old at least.

The third myth is that good schools are produced by good headteachers, so they should be on generously funded PRP.

Of course headteachers, like classroom teachers, have a crucial role in producing good schools. However, good schools can probably stand the odd bad head. We can argue for paying heads more to attract high-fliers into schools but that argument stands without reference to PRP. The fact is that PRP fails disastrously for both headteachers and teachers because it takes so many years to make a real difference when the input/output cycle is so extended.

The fourth myth about PRP is that it will be enough of a carrot (and the refusal to award it enough of a stick) to encourage harder, longer, more effective work. On the contrary, the poor long-term basic pay prospects are a disincentive for many able graduates.

It is true that teachers, just like their students, need long-term motivation. But what sustains 35–40 years of service is teachers' love of young people and their company; the pleasure of watching understanding come as a result of enthusiastic, deft teaching; and satisfaction from sharing in the creation of independence and enrichment of life that education alone can give to the young.

The truth is that this sense of professional pride is the only motivational wave worth riding. Jump off it on to the ripple of PRP and the real power-source of the enterprise is lost.

The final myth is that all the above arguments are 'special pleading', that there is nothing special about managing teachers, and that PRP will bring it home that society expects results from the billions it spends.

Teachers are not unique, but the professions working with people are different, in terms of both motivation and results. This is acknowledged in the vast body of non-educational management literature on organized effectiveness, managing for quality and the place of rewards. Research confirms what teachers (and most parents) instinctively know: when the 'product' is as complex as well-informed people, effective schools or efficient teaching techniques, and wherever internal motivation is the real dynamo, then managers must *not* attempt to tie financial rewards to specific indicators.

Of course we need measurement, we need effectiveness, we need efficiency; we need better ways of assessing mid- to long-term effects. But we need PRP as little as we need other inappropriate, counter-productive, anti-vocational, anti-research paths to mismanagement – and both the theoretical literature and the real world clearly tell us so.

Bruce Douglas is principal of Branston School and Community College and author of a book on quality control mechanisms.

20
A new head

How does a new head start the job? Here, Hugh Figgess explains how he spent his first few weeks as a headteacher.

I became a new headteacher in a school where my predecessor was a skilled, confident and experienced head. It had also just had an OFSTED inspection, which provided a free audit with nothing at stake for me – an opportunity to be totally objective.

When I first arrived there were not too many demands on my time (it did not stay like this for long). I used this period to carry out further audits – one was to interview all staff; the teachers individually and other staff in groups. I asked three questions:

- What is good about the school?
- What needs to develop and to change?
- What do you expect from me?

This was the best thing I could have done. It gave me the chance to get to know people quickly, get to know where they stood and praise what was already good about the school.

The response to the third question was the most interesting; varying from nervous downward glances to long lists for me to deal with – preferably in the following two weeks.

I also spent as much time as I could just walking round the school, calling into classrooms, trying to pick up a feel for how the school worked.

Within five weeks of arriving, we began to review the current school development plan and the information gathered from the other audits was put into the melting-pot. During the next few weeks the updated plan, which was to provide a new lead for the school, began to emerge. At this stage I needed to have a clear idea where I was in the change process:

- Was I at the front leading the troops?
- Was I guiding the leadership of others?
- Was I listening, supporting, directing?

It was, of course, a combination of all three – which is how it should be. It is also a question of maintaining balances, what to change, what to prioritize and what to leave alone.

It was really important, in my view, to make early symbolic changes – pointers to the future – to gather confidence and support cohesion. I chose changes that were fairly certain to work and make a difference quickly.

It was also important during this time to be open, honest and own up to errors. Try to conceal them and you nearly always get found out (I know from the past). I did my best not to make too many and undermine confidence – I did not want the staff to think I was a blithering idiot too soon.

I had to remind myself many times that it was a new school only six years ago. Many staff were there at the beginning and could have felt they had a lot at stake.

Early on, in a fairly large meeting, I discovered one of the guiding principles that the school was built on. I was unwittingly questioning it at the time. If the earth could have opened, I would have been happy for it to swallow me up.

Purposeful change does not come easy; easy change is not likely to be real or sustained.

I often viewed myself as being in a maze trying to get to the other side. There are many dead ends, sometimes the hedge is thin and it is possible to push it aside to get through. At other times, the route is impassable and an alternative has to be found.

The job can be hard. There were mornings when I awoke at 5 a.m. It was at these times that I tried to remind myself that the job is about managing change and handling problems – some problems are mine, but mostly it's encouraging others to solve their own problems.

It is vital to praise staff where it is due. It is equally important to find ways of praising yourself or, at the very least, reassuring yourself that you are heading in the right direction.

After two terms in the job, the senior management team produced a list of achievements since my arrival. We also produced a second list of what remained to be done. The second was considerably longer, but the process definitely helped.

A network of support was vital to retain my sanity – the most important came from inside the school where the deputy head and other senior staff provided mutual support.

The regular 'thinking through' sessions with the chair of governors were an essential feature of development.

And local heads were highly significant (forget about competition and market forces), particularly when it came to contextualizing issues within a local or middle school framework.

Contacts within the local education authority must not be underestimated; it is amazing what you can still get free – you only need to know what to ask for. The local inspector can be a source of support, inspiration, direction or just bring you down to earth from time to time. Shortly there will be appraisal, but that is, perhaps, another story.

Checklist for a new head

- At first, listen, watch and learn.
- Interview staff individually.
- Make one or two quick symbolic changes.
- Set in motion a review of the school development plan.
- Be clear about your own role in the changes you set in train.
- Keep up a dialogue with the governors.
- Make friendly links with the local inspector.
- After a reasonable time, take the views of staff on progress so far.

Hugh Figgess is head of Scotchman Middle School, Bradford.

21

A teacher under stress

What makes leading a team of teachers such a challenge is that the degree of personal involvement which teachers have in their jobs means that there is a great deal of sensitivity to criticism. For many teachers, indeed, catastrophic loss of precious self-esteem lies only just round the corner. This article by Gerald Haigh explores, with particular reference to one case, the way in which one experienced teacher came under pressure from parents. The events that followed made unexpected management demands upon his head.

Teachers cry much more often than people outside the profession think. The tale of walking into the Gents and finding a senior teacher sobbing with his head resting on the wall is part of the folklore of the job.

There is a strong case for suggesting that the inner flame of confidence burns with a fragile light. Why else, if not because they need constant reassurance, do teachers constantly talk about their work? Why is it that non-teaching partners are driven to screaming pitch by pub and dinner-table conversation about classrooms and kids?

The ease with which the light can be extinguished, sometimes for good, is further illustrated by the story of the teacher – for this purpose I will call him Ralph – who, months afterwards, was still suffering from painful self-doubt as the result of an incident in the summer term a couple of years ago.

Ralph is an experienced and successful teacher of A level students. One summer, however, immediately after the exams, the parents of all of his A level group complained bitterly to his head, in writing, that their sons and daughters had found themselves inadequately prepared for the exam. They blamed the way the students had been taught, and were worried that their higher education prospects would be unfairly damaged.

The head replied to the parents' letter, including some evidence from the teacher's own records. 'I was relieved that I do still keep a tight file. I could tell you everything I've done on any teaching day.'

This, however, sparked off another, much harsher, letter from the parents which reiterated the original complaints and went on to accuse the head of being patronizing.

What Ralph was faced with now was a concerted campaign which, though deliberately directed over his head, had him, he felt, very much as its target. An interesting aspect of it was that the parents insisted throughout that they were not attacking Ralph's professional competence. For his part, Ralph believes that if you criticize a lesson or a course then you criticize the teacher. His head felt the same way, and made this point forcibly in writing to the parents.

Now the management ins and outs of this are interesting enough. The school was steadfastly supportive, and of course there were fraught meetings, union involvement and so on. What is important, though, in the context of the present discussion, was the devastating effect it all had on Ralph himself, not just as a teacher but as a person with a private life and a set of emotions. As he said early on in his conversation with me, 'When everyone starts saying you're useless, then you start to believe it. I was increasingly beside myself.'

The summer holiday rapidly arrived and, suggested Ralph, 'Some of the others were able to cross the matter off their agenda. But for me not a day went by when I didn't worry. I didn't sleep properly, I was having nocturnal sweats, and I was physically sick. I couldn't face going into the village because I thought everyone was talking about me. That whole period of my life is indescribable.'

It is important to remember here that Ralph was no insecure beginner but a highly experienced A level teacher with a track record of success – which, paradoxically, is probably why the whole thing got to him as it did.

All teachers of exam groups, of course, have a surge of anxiety as results day approaches. Ralph, though, was on the threshold of paranoia.

'I thought there'd be a lynch mob in the car park, so I asked the head to fax the results to someone I knew, who then rang me up. The first candidate had got an "A" and by that time I was in such a state that I really genuinely thought for a moment that it stood for a new category called "Abject failure".'

As the list of results unfolded, though, it became clear that they were excellent with a significant proportion of As and Bs. Every candidate had the scores they needed for their future plans.

Ralph, though, still had to be convinced. 'I rang the school to confirm it. I still thought there'd be a fax from the board saying it was a horrible mistake. Only when another colleague brought the results round to my door and I'd read them three times did I start to believe them.'

What then, do you think? Letters of apology? Flowers? Shame-faced people at the door? ('I watched the letterbox every day.')

Every teacher reading this knows better than that. Even after the governors wrote to the parents suggesting 'that they could alleviate some of the distress by writing a note of appreciation', Ralph says there was virtually nothing doing – certainly no concerted retraction on the level of the original complaint. He knows, in fact, that some parents continued to feel that the good results did not invalidate their complaint or the way it was handled.

So, for Ralph, the pain went on. Many weeks after the events, he wrote, 'I now doubt my ability right across the board. I dread each day. If only I could sort my sleeping out. Last night I woke at two, four and six, and got up feeling exhausted. I'm left with a legacy of low self-esteem. They've stolen a period of my life, and I feel terribly hurt by that. I look at my own kids now and I remember how I snarled at them when I shouldn't have done.'

Quite evidently, Ralph was in need of a rest – others have said the same. But in saying this are we not, somehow, suggesting that he is part of the problem? There are parallels here with the way that schools deal with bullying and the need constantly to guard against the trap of expecting the victim to carry some of the responsibility. Certainly he refused to take time off. 'I wasn't going to be beaten and broken.'

Casting around for someone else to discuss this with, who might provide me finally with something positive for teachers to reflect on, I thought of a head I knew who for twenty-two years has run a large primary school in a very difficult area of East London.

The job, she agreed, has teachers always hovering between elation and despair. 'You lay yourself bare. You are not thinking of protect-ing yourself, because that's counter-productive – every fibre is going for the progress of the child, and that makes you very vulnerable so that the slightest flick hurts so much.'

At the same time, though – and it was for this message that I went to her – that same high level of personal involvement means that there are great emotional rewards to be had. 'When I feel at my worst, I always throw everything in the corner and go back to the children and reactivate why I came into the job, and they have never failed me yet. It's hard to describe the real buzz you get from having even the tiniest involvement in a child's progress – when a child learns to do something quite simple that they couldn't do before. That's what keeps me going.'

22

Management structures

The management structure of schools – particularly secondary schools – is constantly under review. Senior teachers are expensive, and it may be that today's more democratic schools do not need so many of them. Here, Neil Merrick looks at one possible pattern.

A new breed of assistant headteacher is emerging as more schools appoint non-teaching staff to take on part of the deputy's work or experiment with broader, flatter management structures with fewer deputies – or none at all. But according to the head of a school which shed two of its three deputies – and created four new assistant heads – the days of the deputy are far from over.

The School Teachers' Review Body (STRB) ignores appeals from teacher associations to bring back a statutory requirement for schools to appoint a set number of deputies. But heads must now consider delegating more real management tasks, and deputy headteachers' conditions of service have been redrawn to give them a clearer management role.

Camborne School in Cornwall pruned its senior management team in response to a looming budget crisis. One deputy took early retirement while another was made redundant. At the same time, four senior teachers who had been on the highest head of department scale – what was then called the E Allowance – became assistant heads with deputy status. In the view of the head, Derek Adam, the extra whole-school experience the four assistant heads were gaining would benefit them in the long run. 'I feel that I'm training up new deputy heads,' he said.

Schools with hierarchical management structures tend to make teachers experts in a particular subject or year group but that has not been the case with Camborne's four assistant heads. 'They will be able to move through the profession because of the experience they have had,' said Mr Adam.

Camborne, an 11 to 18 mixed comprehensive, introduced a 'wheal' or team system which was crucial to the new structure. Each wheal was named after a Cornish tin mine, represented about a quarter of the school's 1200 students and consisted of a team of teachers with responsibility for different pastoral and curriculum areas.

Originally each wheal was led by one of four E Allowance holders who were also members of the senior management team. 'They were responsible for a group of students across the school. The idea was to try to devolve decision making,' says Mr Adam.

At the time Camborne was given local management in 1990, its senior management team (SMT) consisted of three deputies and the four E Allowance holders. At first all was well. But by 1992, falling pupil numbers, the diversion of funds from secondary to primary schools in Cornwall, and the high salary costs resulting from a preponderance of older, experienced staff were creating budget problems. 'We had enormous stability but there were forward-planning difficulties,' recalls Mr Adam.

Following a staff review, it was agreed to protect the curriculum by maximizing the number of classroom teachers. The senior management structure therefore became a target for change.

All seven members of the SMT were made redundant and invited to apply for one of five new posts. In place of three deputy and four E Allowance posts, there was to be just one deputy and four assistant heads who would have the pay and conditions of service of deputies.

Although the 1988 Education Reform Act requires schools to advertise deputies' posts externally, the new positions were advertised internally and only the seven teachers who were members of the SMT invited to apply. No objections were made to the manner of the advertisements and, according to Mr Adam, the governing body would have advertised further afield if none of the seven candidates had been suitable.

One of the existing deputy heads retained his position while all four E Allowance holders (three men and a woman) were appointed assistants.

By moving on to the heads' and deputies' pay spine, the assistant heads gained about an extra £1,000 per year and were no longer covered by the 1265 hours stipulation in the teachers' conditions of employment.

Each continued to be in charge of a wheal, but their responsibilities were extended to include more whole-school activities. 'They were no longer simply curriculum or pastoral people. Nor were they tied to a particular year group,' says Mr Adam. 'They had to think whole-school for a particular group of students in their wheal.'

The STRB devoted two pages of its 1994 report to the role of deputy heads. The review body said 'deputies can perform an important role, not only in the absence of the head'. But to justify different pay and conditions of service arrangements from the majority of other staff, they needed to have responsibilities delegated to them that were school-wide and of considerable weight.

The report continued: 'In our view there needs to be a clear distinction between the job of a deputy, so defined, and the job of a senior teacher who can be awarded up to five points for additional responsibilities under the new teachers' pay structure.'

David Hancock, salaries and conditions of service officer for the Secondary Heads Association, said in 1994 that an increasing number of schools seemed to be reducing their number of deputies and replacing them in the senior management team with teachers who would have been E Allowance holders under the old pay structure.

The association had lobbied for the reintroduction of a statutory minimum number of deputies, depending upon the size of a school.

'People are beginning to talk about assistant heads or assistant deputies. They're just changing the title a bit,' said Hancock. 'They are putting them on the management spine but not necessarily as high as designated heads and deputies.'

Derek Adams said that Camborne's assistant heads were given deputy status in recognition of their school-wide responsibilities. It was a reflection of the increased accountability, increased workload and ultimate responsibility.

One of the assistant heads was responsible for day-to-day management, financial monitoring and compilation of attendance statistics.

Another was responsible for 14 to 18 vocational education, appraisal, staff and school development planning and the induction of newly qualified teachers.

A third oversaw community education and marketing, while the fourth was in charge of learning support systems and primary liaison. Each wheal became a budget centre and the assistant head and principal teachers in a wheal were able to decide how much money should be spent on curriculum and pastoral areas, as well as recommending how many scale points a newly appointed teacher should be given. 'Most of the wheals spend more money in a year than I do,' said Derek Adam.

The SMT met once a week while the principal teachers met with senior managers at least once every month. The first deputy (as he was officially titled) became responsible – with the support of the relevant assistant head – for examinations, new building planning, curriculum planning, assessment, recording and reporting, and preparing the timetable. He was also to deputize for the head.

'With the extra external demands being placed on heads, I still think there needs to be a deputy,' said Derek Adam. But he was not in favour of a statutory minimum as it would take away flexibility. 'Each school has to play its cards according to its own experience and its own conditions.'

He said that deputies in future would need to be more aware of financial and personnel matters or their role could be taken over by a bursar or non-teaching school manager.

'I think there is going to be a cultural change. Deputies will need much more financial and personnel experience, and heads must make sure that a school can provide the necessary training so that deputies can gain that type of experience.'

23

A school administrator

Changing the management structure may not involve only the teaching staff. The head in Neil Merrick's article suggested that deputies would need to be more aware of finance and admnstration. Another way forward, though, is to appoint an administrative specialist who will take on more of the non-teaching responsibilities now being borne by senior teachers. The experience of one Coventry school, described here by Gerald Haigh, helps to illuminate some of the issues involved.

Since the advent of Local Management of Schools, many secondary schools have wrestled with whether or not to appoint a non-teaching administrative officer who would relieve the senior teaching staff of the muck and money side of running the school.

Just to make the point, here are three episodes culled from the life of a secondary deputy.

For an hour before school she worked on the computer finance module, preparing figures for the management meeting later in the week. At lunch-time she watched meals being served, because the kitchen staff would like another person on the servery at peak times. And in the afternoon she spoke on the phone to the authority about the rights of a teacher who was requesting maternity leave. She is just one of many deputies whose work in recent years has expanded to take in a whole range of responsibilities to do with finance, personnel and site management.

Ian Kershaw, head of Sidney Stringer Community College, a Coventry inner-city comprehensive, is one head who believes that for senior teachers to do this kind of work is neither cost-effective nor necessarily efficient. 'I can't understand why you'd want to pay a senior teacher or a deputy head to spend fifty per cent of their time looking at finance. Deputy heads should be focusing on the teaching and learning – monitoring, demanding, expecting.'

Pat Nesbitt, one of the school's two deputies, agreed. 'Going down into the basement with a torch to look at the boilers is not my idea of how I should be spending my time. Our focus as deputies is on teaching and learning in the classroom, and we are all committed to that view.'

Put like this, the case seems to make itself. All the same, in the early days of admin officers in state schools, numerous mistakes were made. Typically, a board of governors would panic at the prospect of their financial responsibility and assume that this was where they needed help. As a result, a school would appoint a finance officer only to find that there were lots of other non-teaching jobs to be done. This was how a hapless, newly appointed accountancy-skilled 'bursar' might find himself being expected to tame a caretaker who had been running wild for years.

Another cause of misunderstanding, usually brought about by inability to pay a decent salary, was to appoint at too low a level in the hierarchy, so that the admin officer was just senior enough to cause resentment among existing support staff but too junior to fight their corner at management level.

Ian Kershaw has kept out of both traps. Not only is Peter Holmes, the school's admin officer, a full member of the senior management team along with the two deputy heads, but he has enough experience and expertise to cope with everything from reassuring a meeting of restless cleaners to preparing a set of tender documents for a major building project.

Peter Holmes came to the school nine years ago after a thirty-year career in local government. Although his salary, which is based on local government professional grades, is less than that of many senior teachers, he regards himself as fortunate to be doing the job which he now has. 'I haven't a lot of paper qualifications, but I've picked up a wealth of knowledge without a great deal of formal training. I get enormous satisfaction from this job, and I think I'm well paid for what I do.'

Significantly, Peter Holmes takes finance – the problem area for many teachers – in his stride. 'If you're on top of the finance, it's all structured. It's in place and it should be working – and we're spoon-fed by the computer system anyway.'

Managing people, on the other hand, he sees as much more

challenging. 'It's much less clear-cut, and there are different issues from day to day.'

Peter Holmes is direct line manager to twenty-four people, and meets their four section heads – the senior resources technician, the senior caretaker, the person in charge of the office, and the senior information technology technician – formally once a week. He has no management oversight of teaching staff, but he looks after their personnel issues – salary enquiries, for example. One reason why this part of the job is difficult is that many of the support staff, although responsible to the admin officer, also take operational instructions from teaching staff. Asked for a day-to-day example of how these boundaries overlap, Pat Nesbitt and Peter himself both came up with the same account of how the resources technicians, overwhelmed by a sudden surge in demand from teachers for photocopying, came to Peter to ask for some sort of booking system to be introduced.

The real point of this story, though, is that because Peter is a member of the most senior policy-making group in the school, he was able to get their problem both aired and solved in quick time.

This direct line to the heart of the school will be recognized as a golden asset by those support staff members who have known the frustration of, for example, trying to engage the attention of an overworked deputy who does not clearly understand the problem anyway. The result of having support staff so well led and represented, explained Pat Nesbitt, is that they are in tune with the school's philosophy. 'So if a teacher wants to rearrange a room, or add display boards, it's seen as being for the benefit of children, and not just a teacher being fussy.'

Talk to Peter Holmes and his senior teacher colleagues and you suddenly realize that the strength of the arrangement lies in a contrast of perceptions. To a teacher, while the classroom task is manageable and satisfying, the administrative side of life is usually irksome and worrying. Peter Holmes, however, not only finds satisfaction from being good at the administrative work, but is able to take great pride in being able to provide the right working conditions for pupils and teachers. 'My view – my support staff rule if you like – is that while our equality of status within the organization is not questioned, we are here to provide the quality of support which will allow our professional colleagues to do their job better.'

Ian Kershaw is in no doubt about Peter's importance. 'If I had to choose between losing a deputy head or the admin officer then I would keep the admin officer.'

Checklist

- Get the basic job description thrashed out in advance.
- Financial know-how may not be the most important skill. The ability to manage other support staff is at least as crucial.
- Do not expect Rolls Royce service on a Lada salary.
- Be clear how the new role affects other office staff, and prepare them accordingly.
- Including the administrative officer in senior management has distinct advantages.
- Be prepared to clear up 'overlaps' between the adminstrator's line management of support staff and the right of teachers to give operational instructions.

Part Three
Managing The Premises

For many headteachers, the school building and its services are a burden which has to be borne – a distraction from the business of teaching. It is, though, a responsibility that cannot be shirked, because good management in this area can save money which can then be spent on staff and textbooks. In the articles that follow, writers and experts share ideas about the efficient care of the hardware of educational life.

24
Telephone systems

The telephone is both a nuisance and a godsend. A good system in a school, though, can make everyone's job easier, as this article by Gerald Haigh explains.

In her autobiography, *Smiler Remembers* (Pentland Press), Reta Wrigley tells how Delaval Secondary Modern School, in Northumberland, where she taught for twenty-six years, housed a wartime Air Raid Post. 'It was manned day and night and a telephone had been installed. When the war ended, Mr Soulsby asked if the school could retain the telephone, but his request was refused . . . Any necessary calls had to be made from a public call box about a hundred yards down the road.'

In common with most other schools, Delaval had to wait a few more years for its telephone. Once that first phone was in, things often went unchanged for many years. Hugh Burkinshaw, of Peel Park County Primary in Lancashire, remembers that when he took his post in 1984, 'We had just one black bakelite telephone in the head's office.'

Now, by contrast, things move very quickly. At Peel Park, the single phone has been replaced by three lines serving thirteen extensions, a fax machine and a payphone. And clear on the horizon – nearer, if you have the money to spend – is a world where the phone line is not just a speech carrier but a multimedia highway.

Today's telephones are cleverly designed to appeal to the gadget lover in all of us. This is why we forget the obvious point that the more we have of them, and the easier they are to use, the more calls we will make and the bigger will be the quarterly bill. A primary school today will commonly spend £100 a month on phone calls. How many pennies, I wonder, did Delaval School staff put in the slot of that phone box?

It is very important, therefore, for schools to make sure that any upgrading of the phone system not only fills a real need, but offers some efficiency savings.

That being said, progress has been so fast in recent years that many heads and teachers, still using a thirty-year-old system, may well be unaware of what modern telephones can do. Here are just a few of the possibilities. (Some of these have on the face of it been around for a long time. Modern technology, though, makes them cheaper, and easier to use.)

- Multiple lines. Peel Park has three. Hugh Burkinshaw (and this is a useful tip that some heads might have missed) uses the fax line as his own personal line for outgoing calls, which means that he almost always has a line available. 'Previously, I would have trouble when the phones were busy. I'm an easygoing chap most of the time, but it would get to me and I was tending to emulate John Cleese at times.'

- Extensions. Depending on the system you buy, you can have as many as you want. Peel Park, with 600 pupils, has thirteen extensions. 'We've senior staff around the school who need access to telephones and before, it meant that the office staff had to judge whether to fetch them for incoming calls.'

- Call barring. Some users want extensions that either will not make outside calls, or will only make local ones. Barring is possible at any level. At Rodborough School in Godalming, for example, there are forty extensions many of which are barred from all but 999 calls. One extension, in the sports hall within easy reach of pupils, is set so that it only works at selected times of the day. All of this, explained bursar Jennifer Leigh, can be organized from the office. 'There's a large digital screen with an idiot guide that tells you what you have to do next.'

- Controlling costs. A modern system may automatically route long-distance calls through a cheaper network. It may also offer, through optional features, as much monitoring of costs as you want. You could, for example, have a detailed printout of the calls made from every extension. This, incidentally, makes it easier to recover the costs of private calls. 'I've found it jogs people's memories,' is how Jennifer Leigh tactfully puts it.

Both Rodborough and Peel Park have payphones as part of

their systems. The cost of calls can be set by the school, but Hugh Burkinshaw points out that 'You pick up quite a bit of revenue without setting it to extortionate rates.' In fact a pay-phone set at the same rates as public ones will make money for the school and is a convenience for pupils, parents, visitors and contractors working on the site. (It has to be said, though, that some schools have found that a payphone invites thieves.)

- Nobody in the office? Outside office hours, the system can be set so that incoming calls will ring an extension – or all of the extensions. Thus, when Hugh Burkinshaw comes into school at 8 a.m. and walks off round the building, he can pick up an incoming call from whichever phone he happens to be near. 'And at breaks and lunch-times when the office isn't manned, the same night bell goes on. We have an unofficial house rule here that the phone will never ring more than three times before someone picks it up.'

- Paging. If the extension phones have small loudspeakers you can page people through them. And on some systems you can leave messages on the phone's digital display.

- Cordless extensions. These are digital handsets, a bit like mobile phones and smaller than the cordless phones you have at home. One Coventry primary school went for a BT system with two normal extensions and one cordless phone instead of having ordinary extensions all over the building.

- Interrupting a caller. If the head at Rodborough is on the phone, the office staff can quietly interrupt, unheard by his caller, to tell him that his visitor has arrived.

- Future-proofing. This is important. Dave Rzeznik, at Spinney Hill Primary in Leicester, bought a system with seven extensions, but it has the potential to take thirty. 'Some suppliers were trying to sell us outdated equipment. We wanted something that we could keep adding to.'

One dealer said that he routinely queries any school asking for a very basic system that cannot be expanded beyond, say, two lines and eight extensions. And if you can see, somewhere down the line, big-screen video telephones in the classroom, linking children to their 'pen pal' school five hundred miles away, then you want to know that you can achieve this without throwing everything out and starting from scratch. In this regard the future lies with digital systems. Analogue systems, using older technology, may be cheaper and quite adequate for a school on a limited budget. They are not fully future-proofed, though.

- Why the sudden interest? Digital technology means that phone systems have become all-singing, all-dancing tools for internal and external communication. Because costs can be monitored, users do not experience big increases in bills, and there are real savings in management time. There is dramatically less fetching and finding of people and a big drop in the taking of 'I'll get her to ring you back' messages. And if a new telephone system means that heads become less likely, in Hugh Burkinshaw's words, 'to emulate John Cleese', then everyone's blood pressure will benefit.

How much?

Generalization is difficult, because installation and wiring will vary, and every system offers a wide choice of optional features.

David Rands of Ansamatic, the supplier of Rodborough's system, told me that 'The least expensive system we have ever put into a school was about £1,000. The dearest was £15,000. Most are probably between £3,000 and £6,000.'

Leasing is available, usually at about £60 a quarter per £1,000 of value, over a seven-year lease, although apparently few schools choose it.

Peel Park and Rodborough both have Panasonic DBS (Digital Business System) equipment. Peel Park's was supplied and financed by the authority. Rodborough's came from Ansamatic, a local dealer. Spinney Hill has a BT Meridian system, which can run various combinations of corded and cordless extensions. There are systems by other telecommunications firms, such as GPT, and many dealers offer a range.

25
Improving the office

School improvement has many facets. In its most literal sense, it can mean making the building and its furnishings look better. Many schools can be seen to have done this, for a number of reasons: pride; putting on a better face for parents; improving the working conditions of staff. Local Management of Schools has driven many office improvements – not only by releasing funds (in well-funded schools) but by making it necessary to find room for computers, extra files and sometimes extra office staff.

This article by Gerald Haigh looks at how some schools have improved their office accommodation.

Classrooms, give or take a computer or two and the fact that teachers cannot any longer afford to triple mount their display work, look much the same now as they did thirty years ago.

So, and perhaps ironically, if you really want to see the monuments commemorating the educational revolution, you have to look in the school office. Many longer-serving teachers will recognize the description, by Sybil Collings, head of St Andrew's GM Primary in North Weald, of her school office in pre-local management days. 'When I arrived there was one very old typewriter, an old teacher's desk, and bits of classroom furniture filled with old forms and correspondence.' Now, though, North Weald's office is home to an administrator and two clerical assistants, and there are three networked computers as well as an array of filing cabinets, smart desks and purpose-built seating.

Every school in the land, in fact, has had to look at its office arrangements in recent years. Even the many heads and governors who are reluctant to spend money on administration have had to consider how to accommodate an office computer, a decision with inevitable further effects on desk space, storage and seating.

There have been other pressures, too. Worries about security have caused schools to see whether the office might be given a sight line to, and control over, the school entrance. And running parallel has been a growing awareness of the need to be welcoming to parents and other visitors.

Gradually, then, there has grown, in the minds of many heads, an idea of what the school office should look like – an adequate space, efficiently used, attractively furnished and decorated. It would provide a good working environment for hard-pressed and loyal administrative staff – and, importantly with the growth of competition for pupils, it would give the school a well-made-up public face.

This, essentially, was the vision that formed in the mind of Eddie Woods when he came to be head of Walton Junior School in Peterborough a few years ago. The school office at that time was in a small room next to the head's office, well away from the school's main entrance. 'I saw the pressure the secretary was working under. We needed to have an efficient and effective office. And I was also concerned about the security of the pupils and the staff. It was clear to me that we should move the office to the main entrance.'

The only sensible space was a rectangular books and reading area close to the main door. It had three walls already, and needed only a partition and a door to make it into a room just about twice the size of the original office. The biggest building job was to put in a reception hatch, looking out into the main hallway. Visitors now come through an outside door and then have to identify themselves at the hatch before the secretary presses a button releasing the lock on the inner door into the school. (This inner door has a coded security lock so that members of staff can use it without bothering the secretary.)

The room itself is provided with two crescent-shaped light oak workstations supplied by a local office equipment firm. These provide a desk surface, and then curve round to give enough space for computer equipment. They are, in fact, modular in that differently shaped units can be married up to them.

There was, though, a deliberate delay before these were installed. Julie Bryan, Walton's secretary, explains that for half a term she worked with her old furniture moved down from the original room. 'I'd recommend waiting. We felt we needed to take time to see exactly what was needed.'

The new office is by no means lavishly equipped – there are two new four-drawer filing cabinets and a couple of tall storage cupboards. The original carpets are still down, and there are blinds at the one external window. The total cost, Eddie Woods reckons, including alterations to the electrical and telephone supplies and decoration, was in the region of £5,000.

The difficulty of assessing the real cost of this kind of work, though, is exemplified by the Walton project. Nobody, naturally, was entirely happy about the idea of the reading area – a valued teaching resource used particularly for special needs work – being annexed by the administration. So, as part of the package deal, space and money were found to convert a children's cloakroom into a new library. The lost cloakroom, in turn, was rehoused in what had been a large and under-used store room. The moral is, of course, that the efficient use of school space has as much to do with relationships and school aims as it does with the measurement of floor area.

Another 'knock-on' cost at Walton stemmed from the security system on the main entrance. Eddie Woods realized that there was no use protecting the front door if all the classroom fire doors remained vulnerable, and so they were all fitted with 'crash bar' locks that cannot be opened from outside.

The Walton project, aside from the fact that the office was moved from one part of the school to another, was relatively modest. There are much more radical approaches. Kilmorie Primary in Lewisham, for example, now has just one open-plan office area for the head, deputy and administrator. Peter Webb, the school administrator, explained that 'The school management decided that what they wanted was to move away from separate cramped accommodation and go for something more open – conceptually as well as physically. Anyone can come in and use the networked system, including parents doing work for the school.'

Now, therefore, instead of separate offices, Kilmorie has an open-fronted area off the entrance hall, with four desks in it. Three small enclosed rooms to the side are used for private interviews or conferences.

The motivation for this quite radical change has been as much philosophical as practical. Head David Morris and colleagues wanted a generally more open school, easier for parents to visit and providing greater access by teachers to the school's information systems. The four computers in the admin area are in constant use by teachers as well as by the head, deputy and administrator.

Many heads, of course, would not countenance losing a personal office. David Morris, however, is not one of them. 'I don't want to be shut in a box. I'm much more aware now of what's happening.'

When he wants privacy for interviews or quiet work he can use one of the three conference rooms, which are also available for other colleagues and for outside advisers such as the educational psychologist.

The whole project at Kilmorie, including building work, has cost about £17,000. 'A lot of money to spend on the office,' acknowledged David Morris, 'but we had very definite philosophical reasons for doing it, and we had saved it from our budget over four years.'

He acknowledges that there are some disadvantages. 'Much more business for the office staff for one thing.' Peter Webb feels that the most obvious problem is the loss of quiet concentrated working time. 'I hadn't expected the amount of disturbance when a child comes with problems and is emotional. With this sort of office the work virtually shuts down when that happens. I think the head, too, sometimes feels that he's being dragged away from the concentration that he sometimes needs.'

Nevertheless, 'You cope with it if you believe in the concept.'

The problem of interruptions, although highlighted by Kilmorie's radically open approach, is probably endemic – though often unrecognized – in any school office modernization. If you give secretaries a 'serving hatch' to the outside world, and make them visible behind a glass partition at the centre of the school's operations, then it is more than likely that they will be increasingly distracted.

This is certainly the experience of Julie Bryant, the secretary at Walton Junior, who compares her working day now with how it used to be when she was tucked away down the corridor. 'There might be somebody coming into the office, somebody at the hatch and the phone ringing. Sometimes I feel I just want everybody to go away and let me be quiet.'

The effect is enhanced by changes in the secretarial task itself. The advent of local management, for example, has brought the periodic need for concentrated and uninterrupted work on the school accounts. Peter Webb copes with this by booking one of the small conference rooms. 'I bring my computer from home and spread everything out in there.'

Walton's Eddie Woods believes heads should realize that a more open approach creates this tension and, as he has done, try to compensate with increased secretarial time. 'I'm guilty myself of passing the office door and saying "Can you just . . .". I have to try and curb that.'

At the same time, the increased importance of, and attention given to, office systems has undoubtedly enhanced the status of school secretaries, who are becoming increasingly interchangeable with office workers in business and industry. (Their pay, sadly, tends not to reflect this, which is a very sore point.)

Peter Webb feels, though, that schools still have things to learn about office systems. 'Some schools are a bit naive about office work. A lot of the procedures are not written down, so when you ask where they are they tell you that they all know them anyway. I didn't have the school folklore and it's been quite horrific.'

He pointed out that school filing systems, for example, often depend on everyone knowing where things are. 'They'll say, "Oh, that's in a little plastic envelope at the back of the drawer." In a family atmosphere you can get by on that, but the education system has to plan for continuity when people come and go. Schools are going to start getting people who are moving from job to job, as they do in other walks of life.'

One answer, he believes, is visibility – a clear, well-labelled and sequential filing system, with a list of files available to everyone. 'Easily accessible, carefully labelled – a very visual system. And there are various other bits of information on shelves. We have a metre of blue ring binders, carefully labelled.' The aim is to have a filing system which does not depend on specialist insider knowledge, but can be understood and used by whoever comes into the office.

Putting a toe in the water

The market for office equipment and furniture is as tempting and profitable as you might expect given that it provides the corner-cutting entrepreneur with an opportunity to sell glossy, expensive and not always adequate products to enthusiastic but inexperienced buyers.

The problem for schools is that as they become more independent, the experienced local authority officer becomes less influential while at the same time more and more suppliers would like a slice of the schools market. All of this leaves heads and governors in an exposed position.

John Baines, a very experienced purchasing officer with Cambridgeshire authority, demonstrated to me just how potentially disastrous are the decisions that schools can make. 'We had a project at a school where a company had been in and quoted to do two offices for £6,000. We got one of our own suppliers in and they did better furniture for under three thousand.'

An independent furniture consultant working in the home counties was not surprised by this. 'Margins range from twelve-and-a-half to one hundred per cent. There are some good profits to be had.'

So how does a school protect itself against paying good money for bad furniture? Sadly there are no easy answers. For one thing, a group of highly experienced people will each give slightly different advice. One told me that schools should deal with manufacturers rather than dealers or suppliers. There are obvious reasons for this. 'Anyone can be a dealer, buying furniture and selling it at a profit,' he said, 'I could print a catalogue, hire a car and go round making myself a thousand or two on each little office I did.'

And yet it is quite possible to find suppliers of long-standing reputation who have held the trust of their customers by dealing fairly and going the extra mile. However, though there are differences of opinion, research among buyers, suppliers and schools does throw up some general principles, which I offer albeit with the understanding that there are always going to be some individual exceptions.

Checklist

- Get outside advice if you possibly can, either from a good local authority officer or from an independent furniture consultant. (There are very few of these around as yet.)
- Judge representatives not by glossiness of suiting and swishness of company car but by their familiarity with school life. 'Just tell me what you want', although it sounds helpful, is actually a much less promising start than 'What do you do with the dinner money?', which shows some knowledge of school life. Try to deal with a firm that has worked with schools for a long time. Ask for background – what school or local authority customers can the representative tell you about?

- Be cautious of catalogues. More and more of our buying generally is going to be done from catalogues, and yet how sensible is it to choose a chair, say, in this way? It is very easy to buy, from a catalogue, a chair that looks fancy and is uncomfortable to sit on.

  The range of adjustments is important here. EC guidelines say you must be able to adjust the height of back and seat, but good suppliers will be able to provide one where you can adjust the rake of the back as well – and this same good supplier ought really to be able to send a chair out for you to try.

- Be cautious, too, of stationery suppliers (either mail order or 'supermarket') who also sell some furniture. The chances are that the range will be limited and that their people may not know enough about the products they are selling.

- Make sure that office furniture is to BS 4875. Ask 'what test level?'. If they say, 'zero' or 'what are you talking about?' then walk away. Furniture for school should be to level five.

- Ask about surfaces. They should be of melamine or veneer. Beware of a phrase such as 'teak effect'. Some schools have bought office desks finished in imitation woodgrain that peels off when you leave it in the sunlight.

- Do not buy furniture that comes flat-packed for you to build up yourself. The common experience is that however well you put it together, it always rocks.

- Do not always buy the cheapest. Experts recommend that you buy products that will last ten years. If you do not, you are giving your successors the kind of budget problems that will affect the education of their pupils. Thus, Sybil Collings is satisfied that now the office at St Andrew's primary is refurbished, 'We won't spend money on office furniture for a long time now, because there are things we need in the classrooms and library.'

- Consider doing what Eddie Woods at Walton did, which was to gain thinking and planning time by working for half a term with the old furniture in the new space.

- Beware of becoming starry-eyed. According to one head, 'Too many of my fellow heads think that if the office looks good then the school must be good.'

26

Front of house

Schools are increasingly aware of their 'front of house' impact. They have paid attention to their brochures and notepaper and 'Marketing' has entered the educational vocabulary. Competition for pupils has a lot to do with this, but there is also a general and genuine desire to put on a friendly face. As Gerald Haigh points out here, when this works well the effects are noticeable and very welcome.

Sometimes, the drive for efficiency goes a little too far. Once, I phoned a school only to be answered not by a person but by one of those electronic voices that only allows you further access if you press certain keys. Eventually, after some juggling with numbers and the 'star' key, I telephonically arrived at the office of the person I wanted. And, would you believe it, he had his answering machine on. Not only that, but it did not ask me for a message – 'I am not available to take your call.' Click. End of story. On your bike sunshine, we're busy here.

Which is all very well, but what happens when an anxious parent phones this school? Someone, perhaps, who had to dash to a payphone during a fifteen-minute break?

To be fair, most schools do very well. A human being answers, for one thing. You ask for someone, and after a friendly greeting, the secretary puts you on hold (Mozart sometimes. School choir occasionally. Why never Charlie Parker?)

'Sorry, she's teaching.'

What happens next significantly affects the caller's impression of the school. At worst, the conversation will end there, because the secretary makes it plain that 'She's teaching' is all you are going to get.

Usually, though, the secretary will either take the caller's number or give some advice about when is the best time to ring again. More than once I have encountered a secretary whose anxiety to please has sent her running off to fetch the person I want to the phone. (Very guilt inducing, this. 'Really, there's no need . . .!' I ludicrously shout into the handset as I hear her feet receding down the corridor.)

Visitors, too, are usually better looked after than they used to be in the days when it was difficult to find your way in and you were likely to end up crashing around in the boiler house or opening the door to the girls' changing rooms. (One London secondary school, I recall, had a door marked 'Visitors Report Here'. It was on the second floor, and you could only find it by asking an adult. The pupils shied away like startled horses if you approached them.)

Now, there is usually a waymarked route from the car park, and where there is not, the pupils are noticeably better at helping. Some, including very young ones, are wonderful at looking after visitors – warm, chatty, helpful. In many cases they have clearly discussed or even role-played this either in assembly or in lessons, and they show real pride in having a chance to do it for real. I have occasionally been borne towards a startled-looking head by a fast-moving body-guard, like Chris Eubank entering the ring.

In secondary schools, visitors more often than not step from the outside world into a reception area. Sometimes there is a table staffed on a rota basis by pupils. Occasionally there is a fully fledged front desk run by the office staff. In one case at least the reception staff wear corporate dress and are ready with printed name badges for expected visitors. Is this a good use of the budget? Only the school itself can decide. What soon becomes apparent is that the open reception desk works best if the person running it has good telephone contact with the rest of the school, plenty of initiative and good knowledge of how the school works.

More usually, contact is made with the main admin office, through a glass-fronted hatch. Again, the crucial moments come after the first greeting. I wonder whether school secretaries or receptionists know just how good it makes a visitor feel when they come smilingly out of the office, bypassing the dreaded sliding window?

Once seated in the reception area, a visitor sometimes has to wait a long time. Schools have many priorities, after all, and the needs of children are unpredictable. Unexpected staff absence can cause problems, too. Sensible visitors understand all of this. In fact if there is a good wall display, some school brochures and some folders of newspaper cuttings, the waiting time can be interesting and productive. The time passes more easily, too, if members of staff stop to say hello and to make sure people in the waiting area are being looked after.

Much of the paraphernalia of reception and telephone answering is, of course, seen as being borrowed from the business world. In my experience, though, firms are no better at all this than schools are. What really matters, it seems to me, is warmth and a genuine desire at all levels to show the organization off at its best. If this is there, then a few simple procedures will see to the rest. As a starting point, then:

1 Draft procedure for dealing with telephone callers, based on observed good practice:
   (a) Answer promptly (a typical local authority target, revealed in local authority league tables, is to answer within fifteen seconds. Modern systems have the technology to monitor this.)
   (b) Monitor calls to extensions from the switchboard until they are answered – no caller should be 'abandoned' on a phone ringing in an empty office.
   (c) If the person being called is unavailable, the switchboard might use any combination of the following:
      (i) Take the caller's details and the nature of the question, and suggest alternatives. Many callers routinely ask for the head when someone else is more appropriate.)
      (ii) Ask if someone can ring the caller back. Take details.
      (iii) Suggest a better time to call.
      (iv) If appropriate, suggest sending a quick fax which will help the caller with the later discussion.
      (v) If the caller is going to ring back, take the earliest opportunity to tell the person who is going to be called.
      (vi) Any member of staff receiving a call intended for someone else should be as helpful and positive as possible.
2 Draft procedure for dealing with visitors:
   (a) If they are expected, either display their names in reception (Visitors Today: 09.30 Fred Jenkins of 'Leather 'em Window Services'. 10.30 The Right Honourable Gillian Shephard MP.) or prepare well-presented name badges. Or both.
   (b) Once a visitor has appeared at the sliding window, someone, rather than continuing to talk crouchingly through the hatch, should come out of the office to continue the conversation.

   (c) If the visitor is asked to wait, say why, and offer refreshment. If the wait is prolonged, provide updates which show he or she has not been forgotten.

   (d) If the wait goes on longer than a few minutes, try to find someone else who can at least talk sensibly round the visitor's query.

   (e) Encourage general 'visitor awareness' among staff and pupils. ('Hello. Can I help? Is someone looking after you? Have you been waiting long? I believe you'll be seeing me later.')

3 Finally, and to be fair: Draft code of practice for people (OFSTED, local authority advisers, councillors, Members of Parliament, university researchers) visiting schools:

   (a) Really try hard to make an appointment first. This makes it more likely that you can see the right person.

   (b) Explain on the phone, or write, or fax, an outline of why you want to visit.

   (c) Arrive on time. Too early can be nearly as bad as too late. But leave time to park (never assume there will be room on the site) and to be directed to 'the other building'.

   (d) Announce clearly and pleasantly your name, the name of the person you have come to see, and the time of your appointment.

   (e) Make every allowance for the pressures of school life, especially in a very small school where there may be only three or four adults. Thus, if you feel comfortable in schools, counter the offer of coffee by offering, in turn, to make it yourself. ('Just show me where the stuff is. Can I make anyone else one?')

   (f) Even if it is not obviously relevant to your visit, ask if you can be given a quick tour of the school. Most heads are pleased to be asked.

   (g) If a teacher gives up break or lunch-time to talk to you, then apologize and say thank you. If the teacher has evidently not had time to get coffee then suggest that he or she does so before you start your talk.

   (h) Do not overstay your welcome. If the business is finished, leave. The school has other priorities.

   (i) On leaving, if you found the atmosphere pleasant and the children friendly, then say so. The head will be pleased, as will the rest of the staff when he or she tells them what you said.

27

The school minibus

The school minibus must be properly managed, if it is to be run safely, reliably and with regard to costs. Here, Gerald Haigh provides a list of management issues which will need to be settled, based on the experience of schools that run minibuses.

Buying

1 Set up a working party who will see, compare and drive at least three competing vehicles.

2 Compare costs, but take time to do this, because the comparison goes beyond simple retail price. You will need to look at running costs which should include depreciation. When listening to sales talk about running costs, remember that most school buses do much lower annual mileages than commercially owned buses.

3 Choice of engine. Most buses now have diesel engines of two to two-and-a-half litres capacity. Occasionally there is a petrol option. Diesel offers better fuel economy, balanced by higher maintenance costs. Turbo diesel offers more power and acceleration, but is costly, slightly noisier, uses more fuel and is arguably not necessary in a school minibus.

4 Seating capacity. There are two basic sizes of van which convert to minibuses. One produces a bus of about twelve seats, while the larger buses usually have fifteen seats. A few manage to provide seventeen seats while still staying inside the basic vehicle's legal load limit. The vast majority of schools want a fifteen- or seventeen-seater because of the better pupil to adult ratio.

5 Luggage. A fully loaded minibus has very little luggage space. There is no boot, and luggage should not be carried loose in the gangways. A luggage rack with a rear ladder is usually available as

an optional extra. Remember that a rack will restrict access to some car parks. A trailer is useful, but costs money, has to be maintained, increases fuel consumption, has to be stored, and complicates driving and parking.

6 Safety equipment. Virtually every bus on the market will now offer lap and diagonal seatbelts and properly certificated safety seats and mountings. Check that the middle front seat has a lap and diagonal belt – sometimes there is just a lap belt here.

Other equipment should include a reversing bleeper and wide-angle vision panel in the rear door. First aid and fire equipment should be fitted and in good order. RAC or AA membership is essential because a teacher with a full load needs quick attention. Changing a wheel, for example, is not nearly as simple as it is on a car.

7 Mobile phone. Some buses offer this as free extra, but a phone is quickly and relatively cheaply fitted in any case. It is valuable not only for calling for help but for keeping in touch with school about arrival times and changes of plan.

8 How to pay? As well as outright purchase, leasing is available, either from independent leasing firms or as part of the supplier's offer. Check the figures carefully and try to arrive at a true comparison with outright purchase.

Running

1 Will there be a limit on mileage? Some schools will not allow the minibus to be used for long journeys, on the grounds that coach or train travel is safer and more comfortable.

2 Driver training. There is no legislation on driver training as yet, but a school would be foolish to ignore the issue. If the local authority has nothing to offer then the Royal Society for the Prevention of Accidents runs a scheme, as do various commercial vehicle training companies.

3 Maintenance. A rigorously maintained schedule is essential, contracted to a fully qualified and accredited firm. It is important that, where there are several drivers, one responsible person drives and checks the bus regularly to detect incipient or unreported faults.

4 Fuel. The best way is to have an account with a local garage, and to use other garages only where necessary. Drivers who buy fuel

out on the road will need proper receipts. Parking the vehicle back at school with little or no fuel in the tank should be forbidden and offenders taken to task.

5 Staffing on the road. Some schools want another adult on board as well as the driver. Others feel this is unnecessary. It may depend on the age of the pupils and nature of the journey. In any event, the question has to be faced and a coherent policy arrived at.

6 Finance. Running costs, and the cost of eventual replacement, have to be met. The school should have a policy on this – are departments to be charged at a cost per mile? Under what circumstances may pupils be asked to pay a contribution? Can the bus be hired out (subject to insurance) either to partner organizations such as the PTA, or to completely separate groups? (One school hires its bus to a commercial vehicle rental firm for the summer holidays.) Should depreciation – and thus the cost of replacement – be included in cost per mile? If so the cost will be high. The alternative is to charge running costs only and meet replacement cost when it arrives, as a new capital item. Whichever approach is used, the decision has to be made.

Basic checklist

- A named senior member of staff should be in overall charge.
- Additionally, there should be an administrator – preferably not a teacher – who looks after the paperwork and bookings, and also drives the bus regularly to check on faults and condition.
- There should be a written minibus policy, governor approved, sufficiently clear to settle most questions.
- Only named and approved drivers must drive. Breach of this, even where no passengers are involved, could be considered a disciplinary issue.
- A logbook should be kept in the vehicle, with columns for mileage, fuel purchase, maintenance and comments on condition. Pressure should be applied to make sure this logbook is carefully kept.

28

A school fire

Schools, as the emergencies services well know, are one of the commonest targets for arson attacks. They are also surprisingly susceptible to accidental fires caused by faulty electrical equipment, or appliances being left switched on.

How does a school cope with the aftermath of a serious fire? Here is how the senior managers at the 1800-pupil St Ivo School, Cambridgeshire's largest comprehensive, coped when, a few years ago, the science block was severely damaged by fire just before Christmas.

The Head

First warning of the fire came when the burglar alarm went off in the police station in St Ives. Police investigated and reported flames in the physics laboratory. They called the fire brigade and the caretakers, who called me. I was on the scene within minutes, where I was joined shortly afterwards by the chairman of governors, Rex Wadsworth.

Originally, I was not going to close the school. But I was told at six or so that heat and light could not be restored until possibly mid-morning. It was then I decided to close the school for that Tuesday. I rang the local radio stations and they put out the news in the 7 a.m. bulletins. They wanted statements so I did a couple then. I had telephoned the deputies and the head of science by now and the other people who needed to be informed: governors and the county. The head of the county's property division was on site by 8 a.m. and the vice-chairman of the county education committee shortly after 9 a.m. The authority's response was magnificent.

I was not aware of taking strategic decisions. It was all instinctive on my part. I did give the deputies clear instructions about the tasks they should concentrate on, but that was pretty obvious anyway with such a professional staff. Everybody used their initiative.

I thought it important to keep staff informed and called a briefing at about 9 a.m., where I said that I was not ruling out arson. We faxed a press release to the local media at the end of the morning with an update in the afternoon. We were very pleased with coverage, especially the headline 'St Ivo School shows its class' over the report saying that pupils would be back at their desks the next day.

I thought it essential to release the science department, both teaching and support staff, to enable them to draw upon their collective memories to compile a full inventory of their losses. Otherwise, I wanted as normal an end of term as possible. The Christmas concert went on a day late, so did the Year 7 carol service. The sixth form lunch for the elderly was held in a local motel, while its Christmas party for the disabled went ahead as planned in school on the Thursday.

Deputy Head 1

Very quickly we decided how we were to manage the day. As I had the premises and property brief, I took over liaison with the local authority. Deputies and senior staff were given clear responsibilities. This made what happened during the rest of the day go very smoothly. A review meeting was then held at the end of the day.

Communications were a top priority. The school's only outside line was jammed with incoming calls, but we were able to use another number in the community education office. It is very important in a crisis to have a line exclusively for outgoing calls.

The county responded magnificently. All the relevant people were in school by 8 a.m. We held a crisis management meeting at 10 a.m. and another the following day. I cannot over-emphasize the importance of holding such meetings for all affected parties (school insurers, loss adjusters, engineering, purchasing officers, inspectors, maintenance staff) so that everybody knows what everybody else is doing. Such a meeting saves much time subsequently.

We did not take too many decisions at the first meeting but we did identify areas where decisions had to be taken. These meetings decided such matters as the demolition of the fire-damaged science block, and the location, erection and fitting out of temporary laboratories.

The reception and office staff responded superbly. We allowed teaching staff to go home if they wished and let the reception staff go in the afternoon as they had come in very early. This was an oversight – we should have kept the telephone manned all day. The head and deputies were the only ones left later on to answer the telephone.

Of the many lessons, perhaps one of the most important is the enormous value of being within a local authority. I wonder what would have happened if we had been a grant-maintained school and had had to deal with the making safe of the site, demolition, provision and furnishing of mobiles ourselves, in addition to all the in-school reorganization, forward planning and support staff? A private organization contacted us and offered to erect mobiles and equip them in three months. In three weeks Cambridgeshire County Council had equipped mobiles in place. The science department thought all its teaching materials had gone up in smoke. They were delighted to find that a file copy of all departmental printing was kept on file for two years by the reprographics department – a lifesaver.

Deputy Head 2

I went off to my office to organize science-teaching room changes for the rest of the term. I shut myself away and worked until 6 p.m. with half an hour off for lunch. I was helped initially by two colleagues who read out the timetables. There were room changes for eleven laboratories and one room. I also had to cover seventeen science staff for the rest of the week. I brought in five supply staff, three of them scientists. I was helped by Year 11 being out of school on study leave for mock exams. It was pretty demanding and exhausting, like doing a massive cover for three days in one go.

Science Co-ordinator

I asked the head to let the science staff meet separately. We all sat down in the careers library and simply brainstormed what we had to do, writing things up on the whiteboard as people thought of them. We then drew up lists of things to do. It was helpful and important that people had something to do. One or two members were particularly shaken. A huge chunk of their lives had gone. The effect is still there.

The magnitude dawned on us. The physics and biology departments were wiped out. Chemistry was little better. There were no buildings, no equipment, no lesson plans. All the lower school's courses had gone, so were all the GCSE records. Lots of personal stuff had gone, both teachers' and pupils'. Fifty pets from the pupils' entemological society had died.

The county acted quickly with the management. We were given £50,000 at once to buy equipment, which we got on with. A mammoth task was to draw up a detailed inventory for the insurers. This included every item in every cupboard, as far as we could remember.

We cannot pretend there will be no effect on pupils. But we are making sure that they do not have to worry about it. We will sort things out. We have lost a great deal of their work, written and practical; almost all the practical assessments they have done, at both A-level and GCSE. The boards are fairly used to dealing with such disasters. We are asking them to accept our assessments.

The first couple of weeks of term are going to be the hardest, since we will have to teach in temporary accommodation without equipment. We are to have nine mobiles, each comprising two classrooms. They will be equipped as laboratories as they arrive.

There is now a feeling that we can start again. The county architect has already drawn up a tight programme for rebuilding which will include two extra laboratories that were already planned.

The bonus that can come out of this is the chance to start again, not merely replace what was there before.

Postscript

St Ivo's brand new science block opened in September 1993.

29
Disaster planning

Every head hopes that a disaster never happens. On the other hand, every head wonders just how he or she might cope if it did. There are also, of course, many events short of tragedy which require prompt and effective emergency action. Based on interviews with people who have had to deal with terrible events, Gerald Haigh looks at how schools might look ahead and think the unthinkable.

Just consider this scenario for a moment.

As deputy head of a school you have a phone call from a school party travelling abroad. The call has come to you because the head is unavailable. There has been a fire at the hotel. The line is not too good – your colleague is in a phone box in the street – and details of your school's involvement are not immediately clear. Perhaps nobody is affected at all, but all the same, stories will soon come back to parents from children phoning home. You try the head yourself, but he is obviously not at home.

Your first instinct is to go to the school, because that will quickly become the focus of attention. It is 2 a.m. Can you get into the school? Can you get into any of the offices? Will you know what to do when you get there? And suppose your colleague phones again while you are travelling to school? In other words, have you and your staff done any contingency planning at all, however sketchy? As you sit there trying to think what to do next, the telephone rings again. '*Evening Post* here . . .'

Distressing and sudden happenings that affect school pupils are not quite as rare as we may think. Most heads will be able to think of something that has happened to a school in the neighbourhood – the death of a pupil or teacher; a serious mishap on a school outing;

major vandalism or a fire; a violent assault on school premises; a traffic accident to a school party.

And there are also, of course, the occasional tragedies that make the headlines – the year 1993 alone saw both the loss of four young canoeists in Lyme Bay and a fatal school minibus crash on the M40.

A recurrent theme in these stories is the way that they seem always to intrude suddenly, and usually by phone, into the middle of the domestic life of a head or a deputy – in Coventry, for example, in 1993, a primary head answered her phone to be told that her school was ablaze. Twelve years ago, in Sandwell, a secondary head took a call which brought the news of a fatal accident to the school bus. Out of school hours, that is how it happens, and it makes for a compelling, heart-wrenching image – the phone rings, a familiar enough event in a busy household, a hand goes out to pick it up, and nothing is ever quite the same again.

Whatever the incident, one thing is certain – the assumption is that as soon as the head is available, he or she will take charge. The burden, obviously, is awesome, and it is clear that the head in this position needs support – quickly, before the conflicting demands of parents, community, media and the need to keep the school running become overwhelming.

It follows that a school would do well, from time to time, to consider how it might respond were that life-changing telephone call ever to arrive. Whether there is a senior staff discussion, or a wider workshop, or simply an informal review, the aim ought to be to ensure that if something serious and unexpected happens, then everyone at least has an idea of what to do. At the very least, enough people should have access to enough up-to-date telephone numbers to ensure that nobody is left unsupported for any longer than necessary.

Of course, for most schools the dreadful call will never come. There are many levels of trouble, however, and for every tragic incident there are many which are merely irritating and expensive and threaten the continuity of learning. When something happens, the school that has braced itself to make a plan, even if it consists only of a 'what if' conversation between senior colleagues, should at the least be able to avoid adding unnecessarily to the pain and confusion.

The longer view

Once the initial emergency has been dealt with, and as time goes on, other needs will become apparent. Pupils and parents may need professional counselling; the authority will help with this, although the school may have its own contacts – if, for example, it is a church school.

Pupils may be deeply affected, often in not easily visible ways, for a long time – right up to exams two years later in one case. One school set aside a room, regularly staffed, to which affected pupils could withdraw whenever they wished. It was used for many months after the incident. Teachers, too, will be emotionally affected, and there will be many of the same dynamics, and the same need for tolerant understanding, as in a bereaved family.

Perhaps most challenging of all for a head is the experience of going to well-meaning fund-raising events in the locality. In the wake of one heavily publicized tragedy the head went to something almost every night for several weeks. He felt strongly that each event deserved his personal attendance, but the effort severely taxed his emotional strength. If it looks as if events are snowballing, colleagues would do well to be assertive in protecting the head.

A distressing or tragic incident takes over a community and becomes the major topic of conversation as well as dictating events from day to day. Sensitive management means allowing this to go on for a finely judged period of time. The moment comes, though, when the page has to be turned. Affected schools all experience this, and find it necessary to decide when to go forward – no more interviews, no more events.

And yet, schools always find that the incident keeps coming back, because as with any bereavement, there are bridges to cross – Christmas, the first anniversary. And then similar happenings in another school, even years later, will bring back memories. It helps, though, to have made the decision to move on.

- Major incidents are rare – but equally unexpected ones that are expensive, disruptive and irritating, and which call for quick and effective management response, are much more common.
- So – think the unthinkable – make it an agenda item.

Practicalities to consider in running a discussion or a 'paper crisis'

- Allocate roles – who will come to school? Who will go elsewhere – to the site of the incident, perhaps, or to hospital? Who will alert other colleagues? Who will deal with the media? Who will be interviewed?
- Involve other colleagues as soon as possible. And in any case keep them informed. Staff will be hurt if they feel shut off from management activity after a major incident that, after all, affects them deeply.
- If you are linked to a local authority, involve them as soon as possible. (Names? Phone numbers out of hours?) However unusual the incident, the chances are that they have some kind of experience to draw on. Experience shows that many authorities are very supportive. A Coventry head whose school burned down had a senior officer at her side from the moment she arrived at the site.
- How accessible is the school building out of hours? Who knows what to do?
- Who knows how to operate the phone system? Listed phone lines may be jammed by incoming calls. Where is there a free outgoing phone line? The chances are you will have unlisted lines dedicated to fax or computers. Or use mobiles – does the authority have some for loan?
- Will parents come and gather at the school? Where will you put them? Who will look after them? Hot drinks?
- Are members of an affected party on their way back to school? How can you arrange for their arrival to be free of unwanted press attention? (Meet the transport out on the road. Police may help. Use a remote gate, a neighbouring school or a village hall perhaps.)
- Try to scotch rumours by giving out facts to the local community early and frankly.
- Deal fairly with the media, and understand their deadlines. They will be intrusive, but may be less so if you give hard factual information as and when you can.
- Protect the head. The head's role is to deal compassionately and unhurriedly with the people most closely involved – parents,

affected pupils – without being distracted into tasks that others can do.

- When there is death or serious injury, remember that however shocked pupils and teachers may be, the school is not as badly affected as are the families. The head of a school affected by a multiple pupil fatality tells of being aware that neither his nor the school's suffering could compare with that of the parents. He felt strongly that the school had no right to 'own' the tragedy, constantly reminding staff and pupils of this, and keeping school events and his own public utterances to a minimum.

  Whether or not this attitude is right, it is clear that a school dealing with a major tragedy ought to have a view about how its own grief lines up with that of parents.

- Once the immediate crisis begins to settle, set up a planning group to look further ahead – counselling, fund raising, memorial events.

- In the fullness of time, agree on a moment to close down media contacts and special events and take the community forward.

Some quotes:

'When I got to the hospital there was a great crowd of people there – police, reporters, parents, the general public. And the only person the parents recognized was myself. People do have expectations of you, and I was quite conscious of that.'

'I realized straight away that the real loss is that of the parents. Although everybody in the school feels a deep sense of personal sorrow and grief, it is only a shadow of what the parents feel.'

'I've been a teacher for most of my working life, and a head for seventeen years, and I never expected that a school matter, however serious, could change my life for ever as this one certainly did.'

'After several weeks of being out four nights a week at fund-raising concerts and events, it became a strain, emotionally and physically. And yet I didn't feel that I could allocate only a certain amount of time to these activities. I just had to go to them.'

30
School security

School security – protection against vandalism, theft or intrusion – has crept steadily up the priorities of heads and governors in recent years. High profile fatal incidents – the murder of a London headteacher in 1995; the dreadful massacre of infants in Dunblane in 1996 – add to the concerns of parents and teachers. Less well publicized, though, is the fact that schools are increasingly being targeted for petty theft. Not only are they likely to be burgled at night or over the weekend, in attacks that may also involve vandalism or arson, but they are very susceptible to daytime walk-in thefts of handbags and petty cash. Heads and governors have to think of all these levels of possibility, and balance risk against cost. Here, Paul Lewis has a guided tour with a police architectural liaison officer, and talks to a head who is trying to keep her children safe on a limited budget.

All schools can improve their resistance to intruders and do so quite cheaply. And anything which makes it hard for strangers to enter a school helps protect everyone against intruders of all sorts and may just prevent a personal attack or an abduction.

Crime prevention is now a high priority with the police. Every force has an architectural liaison officer whose job is to design out crime, to ensure buildings offer minimum opportunities for it, to deter potential criminals and to help successful ones be apprehended.

Sussex is not the inner city, but it has its share of crime. Peter Hardy, the force's architectural liaison officer, arrested the Brighton bombers and has nicked half the criminal population of Brighton in a long detective career. He has just finished a report for five Sussex schools on improving security.

One of them, Varndean School, is situated next to playing fields and overlooks Brighton. At the open entrance gate a stern notice warns visitors that they may committing an offence if they cause a nuisance or disturbance. Without it the head cannot evict people who trespass.

Varndean was built in 1926 for half the 900 pupils it houses today in extended buildings. Once past its formal entrance sign, there are no other clear instructions. A visitor could quite legitimately wander through several open doors into various buildings without coming across the reception office or a clear sign to it.

Peter Hardy took me to the old entrance of the school and explained the importance of signs. 'Signage is cheap and a cost-effective way of improving security. I advised them to move reception here. The entrance is overlooked by the secretary; there is a double door so the inner one could be secured electronically. In that way you control access.'

Headteacher Pam Bowmaker accepts the need for security and is acting on some of Peter Hardy's recommendations, including moving the reception desk. But she is not convinced that she should close all the other entrances. 'With a secondary school, especially in buildings like these, you tend to have more entrances. I have got grave concerns about 900 children going through one door. You have to have a balance, I'm not prepared to make it a fortress.'

Her school is full of doors, including old fire doors. Each will cost £600 to replace, money she does not have. Nor does she believe the government will provide extra cash following the recent report of the Working Group on School Security.

'This year we are in a deficit situation,' she says. 'We get no extra money for this: it is all part of our devolved budget.' So new doors compete not just with other building works but also with books and teachers' pay.

Peter Hardy recognizes that many schools can only afford cheap security solutions. In the corridors of Varndean are large windows with six glazed panes in wooden frames. All of them can be opened. 'The simple solution is to screw those into the frames and leave just some of the top ones for fresh air. And fit laminated glass. It is twenty-five per cent dearer than ordinary glass but is virtually unbreakable.'

Next to them are outward-opening exterior doors. 'You need hinge bolts on those to stop criminals tapping out the pins in the hinges and opening the door from that side. They cost £3 a pair.'

Another of his hobby-horses is what he calls 'natural ladders', objects or design features which give people an easy access to upper storeys or flat roofs where security is often more lax. 'Cast-iron drain-pipes will take the weight of two men: plastic buckles with one. Take them down, sell them for scrap – if you've got one of those fan boxes that'll fetch £40 as an antique – and use the money to buy plastic. If you're lucky you can actually make a profit.'

Next door to Varndean is Balfour Infants School. Built in 1971, the architect clearly thought that deeply recessed doors would protect the building from the strong sea winds. But they also provide havens for criminals to plan their attacks on the doors and for drug addicts.

The school is now building out the worst of these; a new perimeter fence defines the edge of the school's ground and a large reception area is well signed and everyone has to pass through it and get a badge. In other places, fire doors have had Chubb locks fitted, perfectly legal as long as the Fire Service approves the installation and procedures for ensuring they are only locked when the building is empty.

But there are still things to do. A television and video is carefully locked to a stand. But the stand is loose and on wheels. 'I nicked someone wheeling one of those out of a school round here,' says Peter Hardy.

He is critical of the pleasant greenery close to the buildings. 'I like plants as much as the next person. But that's just giving a hiding place for abductors, thieves and vandals. Cut it back. Plant trees with clear sight lines below three feet. And that bollard, gate and flat roof give one of the best natural ladders I've seen.'

That problem too is being addressed by headteacher Jane Quincey. But money is limited. Would she consider sponsorship? 'We put £1,000 a year into a health and safety fund and this work all comes out of that. If it's not enough, well, five years ago I would have said "no" to sponsorship. Now I'd have to discuss it.'

Peter Hardy has the co-operation of the local authorities and is asked to comment on all larger planning applications for new or refurbished buildings. His standards for design of schools have been adopted by East Sussex County Council. But even so, buildings of which he is highly critical are erected.

We visited another school which has just spent a great deal on refurbishment and new building. Peter thinks the designer got it wrong. There are plastic and aluminium skylights ('forty-five seconds and you're in'), louvre windows in a room with a hi-fi system ('they're useless'), a movement detector that did not detect us for nearly four-fifths of the length of a corridor ('it should have been tested') and external doors that are recessed and 'they've got no hinge bolts'.

In another school we saw computers clearly visible on the ground floor of a building clearly labelled Information Technology Centre ('that tells villains where they are'). We saw a waste bin by a wall ('a natural ladder to the roof').

'I don't want you to say I am critical of architects. They design for their own purposes. But you can design crime out of buildings and we've proved it. In many ways this is the most satisfying job I have had.'

What annoys Peter is that with a bit of thought these things could be put right easily and cheaply. Although he claims not to consider the financial aspects of making schools secure, he knows the environment he is working in. That is why he did not recommend closed circuit television to any of the schools. They just could not afford it. His mission is to get teachers and architects thinking of security in all their plans.

Checklist: Inexpensive ways to improve your security

- Perimeter fencing should be transparent to allow passive surveillance by neighbours, passers-by or police.
- Signs should be erected: clear warnings at the entrance, one clear route to a single reception point.
- All visitors must sign in and be given a badge. Pupils should be told to report any adult without a badge to a teacher.
- Apart from the main entrance, all other exterior doors should be self-closing and, where possible, locked.
- Alarms should be fitted to prevent exterior doors being opened.
- Exterior doors need hinge bolts. All locks should meet the British Standard – at least a five-lever mortice lock.
- Recessed doors should be built out level with the building line.
- Fire doors need locks or steel plates.
- Glass accessible from outside should be 7.5 mm laminated.
- Reduce the number of opening windows.

- In older schools with wooden frames, windows can simply be screwed into the frames.
- Louvre windows should be replaced.
- Exterior lighting should be controlled by sensor or timer and illuminate vulnerable areas.
- Greenery and plants should be cut back to leave clear sight lines to the building, especially doors, windows and flat roofs.
- Natural ladders – waste bins, cars, fences, drainpipes, high ground – should be removed. Anti-climb paint can help.
- Burglar alarms and panic buttons should be fitted and sensors must cover all the areas to be protected. If the school is used in the evenings, only de-alarm booked areas.

Part Four

Information
Technology

31

Computerized administration in school

When computers first appeared in schools, in the late 1970s and early 1980s, it was assumed that they would chiefly be employed in the classroom as learning aids. A few schools used them for such administrative tasks as library cataloguing, but by and large the school office computer was rather slow to appear.

Now, though, virtually every school has a computer in the school office, and heads take it for granted that there are some jobs which the computer will do best. Gerald Haigh here covers a number of points intended to clear up some misconceptions and to indicate how things might develop.

Crossing the boundaries

Up to very recently, the office computer has been used for admin, the classroom computers for the curriculum – a position reinforced by the use of fundamentally different systems and machines in the two areas. Lately, though, the boundaries are being crossed. Pupil record files, for example, should be accessible from the classroom by the teacher, and the phrase 'curriculum management' implies that the two areas are not always separate. The growth of systems which can be used in both areas is helping, as is the increasing belief that it is fundamentally inefficient to have two incompatible systems in a school.

Big systems

The schools market has encouraged software suppliers to develop 'modular' systems for schools. Such a system will have at its heart a list of the pupils, with as much supporting information as is appropriate – addresses, dates of birth, teaching groups, year groups and so on.

This database of information can then be manipulated to produce class lists, year lists, exam entry lists – any kind of pupil list which is required. This facility alone is extremely helpful, and makes very easy many tasks which school secretaries have for many years had to do laboriously with typewriter and Tipp-Ex. A comprehensive administration system will also have a staff database, and a finance module which helps the head with budgeting and accounts. There may also be a library module which will use the core pupil database so that lending and borrowing can be recorded electronically on the computer in the library.

Timetabling

The writing of a computer timetabling system is a specialized art, and some suppliers of modular systems do not attempt it, but buy in the timetable module from another supplier. There are also well-proved free-standing timetable systems, but these should be capable of taking data from the central pupil database.

The task of sorting out option groups, as secondary pupils make choices for exam courses, can also be done by computer. This is related to timetabling, and the same specialists who supply timetabling systems may also offer option systems.

The usual assumption is that it will be quicker to do timetabling or option groups on a computer. However, users report that time saving is not always as dramatic as anticipated. The real advantage is to do with the number of choices. A teacher using a manual system may well simply plump for the first solution that works, and not feel inclined to look further. A good computer timetabling or option system, though, makes it easy to explore lots of alternative ways of solving a problem. The system offers the alternatives; the choice is still for the teacher to make.

Registration

A computerized school office will already have all the pupils listed on the computer. It seems an easy step to use this list as the basis of an electronic attendance register. The great advantage of doing this is that all the attendance data is then in the computer ready to be handled and printed out in whatever form is necessary. A big return of attendance figures to the government becomes as easy as letting an enquiring parent know what Jimmy's attendance record for the term looks like, or as allowing a year head to find patterns of absence – two pupils always away together; a child always away on games day.

The advantage of computerized registration data, therefore, is not in dispute. What does cause schools to scratch their heads is the challenge of getting the data from the point of collection – which is in the classroom, twice a day – into the computer down in the office. The teacher's paper register is clear, and easy to use. Any other system must be equally easy. Here are some alternatives.

1 Keying in manually. An office worker collects all the paper registers, calls up corresponding electronic registers on the computer screen, and copies the data from paper to computer. There are disadvantages – not least that by interposing another manual operation, errors become more likely. There is also a time penalty – data is not available until the keyboard operator has finished. The operator also, obviously, costs money.

 However, these disadvantages can be overstated. A good operator who does the job regularly becomes fast and accurate – in one school the whole task was done in twenty minutes by a keyboard operator who doubled as the receptionist. (And remember that it is only necessary to enter absences.) The wages costs are not great, given that every system costs money, and some cost a very great deal. This manual method can also be used to gain thinking time during which the school management look at other kinds of data entry.

2 Optical mark reader. The teacher marks not the traditional paper register but a specially made OMR form. This is taken to the office and put through a mark reader which converts the pencil marks straight into computer data.

 The disadvantage here is that the paper forms have to be taken down to the office, and carefully handled so that they are not damaged or creased to the extent that they will snarl up the reader. Some schools have real problems with this. Others report no trouble at all. Determination and strong management may well be the answer here.

The advantage of OMR entry is that it can be very cheap. This is because many schools already have most of what they need to get started – a computer software system which includes a registration module, and an optical mark reader which they had for assessment data entry and which stands idle for much of the time.

3 Swipe card. Each pupil carries a card – either with a magnetic stripe or with a bar code. The pupil 'swipes' in a card reader as he or she comes into school, and the data is automatically transferred to the office computer.

The disadvantages are fairly obvious and are to do with the reliability of a system which depends on the co-operation of pupils. Nevertheless, there is plenty of evidence that some schools make swipe card registration work well, and teachers in such schools will typically insist that the disadvantages are overstated, and that it is not fair to mistrust pupils before giving the system a try. The answer, probably, is to do with the nature of school buildings, the number of entrances and swipe points involved, the degree of supervision possible, and the overall disciplinary ethos of the school. Some heads who run swipe card systems obviously believe that a school unable to make such a system work clearly has problems which go beyond the simple business of registration.

4 Radio link. In this system, each teacher taking registration has a small computer radio linked to the office computer. Just before registration, the teacher calls up his or her group's register from the office. It appears on the small computer and the teacher marks it, then sends it by radio link back down to the office. The advantage of this is that the data is very quickly into the system, and it also cuts out the physical movement of paper from classroom to office. And unlike a swipe card system, it puts control in the hands of the teacher. It does, however, cost a lot of money. Nevertheless, there are plenty of schools and colleges who feel that the efficiency savings balance the outlay.

5 Using the network. A few schools have a networked computer in every classroom. Some schools are close to it. The obvious answer for them is for teachers to mark the register on the network. Even

if the network has to be extended a little to make it work, this could be at least as cheap as some of the other options.

6 Future possibilities. Pupils may wear a small electronic button which can be read as they pass a sensor. Further on, it will be possible to identify pupils by pointing an electric camera at them.

Systems such as this, though, can start to look like electronic surveillance – something which many teachers simply would not like. There are obviously some decisions waiting to be made in this area.

Checklist:

Buying information technology for the school office

- There is always more than one supplier. Do not just go for the same system that the school down the road uses. Investigate the options properly.
- Remember that a quick demonstration may well confuse. You must take time to investigate what the system will do for you in your school. Set up an IT advisory committee, made up of representatives of all the interest groups in the school.
- Remember also that a pretty screen does not always mean that the system is a good one.
- Ease of use is obviously a factor. But it is still true that some highly efficient systems take time to get to know. If a specialist package – handling finance, for example – is going to be used regularly by one person, who will gradually become an expert in it, then the system's fundamental efficiency is more important than whether it is easy to learn.
- What about training? Are training costs included in the buying package? How much training is needed? Who will need it?
- What about support? The old saying about information technology is that only three things matter – support, support and support. Can you phone? Will someone answer? Will someone come out?
- Is the person making the decision the same one who will be using the system? Is the head going to choose a word processor for the secretary to use? Is that sensible? This is where the IT advisory committee comes in.
- What are the implications for management and organization?

Computerized registration, for example, will bring changes to the school office, and to the tasks of people such as year heads. All of this needs to be thought out in advance, but with enough flexibility to accommodate the unexpected – for example, one member of staff may demonstrate an affinity for IT, while another seems unable to take it on. Sensible adjustment of job descriptions may take care of this.

- Garbage in, garbage out. This is another information technology cliché. You must have clarity about the process you are going to computerize – for example, before you computerize registration, you may well want to be clear about the following:

  1 Who is authorized to make changes to a register when a pupil arrives late?
  2 Who can add reasons for absence when they become known?
  3 Who handles absence notes, and where are they kept?
  4 Under what circumstances will a phone call from a parent be acceptable, and when would you want to ask for a letter?
  5 When is a pupil counted as 'late'? And who has the authority to amend this in individual cases?

  Surprisingly many schools are vague about some or all of these. Tidy them up before going to a computerized system, or you may end up blaming the system for problems that lie deeper.

- Consider how you introduce the system. Rarely, if ever, can you just bolt it on to the ordinary working life of the school. Someone has to try it out, and they need time in which to do it. Will you need a pilot scheme of some sort? Will staff need to be convinced of the need to change their method of working? (Schools can, and do, underestimate the staff resistance factor, with disastrous results.)

32

Computer admin: The head

How might information technology impinge on the way that various people in school organize and manage their work? In the following articles, Gerald Haigh looks at how a head, a school secretary and a classroom teacher might be helped by computers.

The head

There are three sorts of head. One proudly points out to visitors that there is no computer terminal in his or her room. Another has a state of the art machine but nobody has ever seen it showing anything other than the main menu screen. Yet another spends all day hunched, back to the door, over a terminal which is in constant use.

Nobody, of course, has the right to say which is the correct role model – the place of IT in the life of the headteacher is not yet well enough established. What is certain, though, is that information technology is only going to make real progress – whether in the office or the classroom – if the head shows real interest and involvement.

Support from the head is particularly important in the early days, when systems are being introduced and everyone is frustratedly throwing things at the screen and crying out for the return of older and better times. This is when, according to IT consultant and former Northamptonshire secondary head Alan Conchie, 'The senior management team has to have a clear vision of what can be done, and will support it through thick and thin even when it's struck by lightning.'

This presupposes that the head will have enough knowledge of computers to be able to discuss the issues, if not the actual technology. Alan Conchie agrees: 'I don't see any answer other than senior management having a degree of IT literacy.'

What, though, does he mean by 'a degree'? Many heads will be relieved by Alan Conchie's insistence that 'It certainly doesn't involve putting data in. No senior manager should be doing this.' Quite apart from its being a waste of a highly paid person's time, the last thing any administrator wants is a computer-buff senior manager who stays behind in the evening altering the data in the system.

What the head must have, he suggests however, is a good understanding of what each bit of the school's management system will do – 'the ability to say, "I know it's possible to do this, and I want it done."'

Just because the head is not putting figures and names into the system does not mean, though, that he or she has no need to operate the keyboard. At the most basic level, it really is an advantage if the head can produce a budget printout, or a class list, or a pupil's attendance record without having to ask a secretary.

In this sense the head's needs may be different from those of the specialist operator of the admin system. The administrator wants an efficient multi-level suite of software that goes wider and deeper than anyone is likely to travel, and is powerful enough to tackle all the jobs, including the ones that nobody has thought of yet. It may be difficult to learn, but then anything worthwhile probably is, and provided the training is good and there is efficiency and speed in the long term, the early frustrations will eventually be overcome.

Heads, though, probably just want to use bits of the system, at irregular intervals. Its maze of highways and byways is just too confusing – secretaries may show them how to get some budget information up on the screen for the chair of governors but a month later, when the chair comes in again, they have forgotten what they did. What they long for, therefore, is something with a friendly-looking front end – easy to use menus, on-screen prompts and memory-jogging icons. They do not want to know how to order nineteen dozen toilet rolls from Yorkshire Purchasing, but they would like to be able, with a couple of mouse clicks, to see how much money the school has spent on toilet rolls this year.

This is why heads like the look of recent systems running under Windows, which at least makes complicated software look easier to use.

Heads also like to take bits of the admin system home, or to different parts of the site, which is why so many of them now have laptops. Andrew Gilroy, a Warwickshire primary head, was quick to see the advantage of adding a laptop to the standalone PC with which his school was originally equipped to run local management software. 'I have the facility to take away information about children. I can also write letters at home. It's a good time-saver.'

Some heads have found that giving out two or three laptops to senior members of staff is a quick and easy alternative to installing an admin network – and the network can still come eventually, when everyone has had time to consider what to buy.

But whether or not the head has the latest PC on the desk and goes home every night with a laptop and portable printer matters less than a clear demonstration of belief in, and commitment to, the idea that IT will repay the initial time investment many times over. As Alan Conchie says, 'The worst situation of all is where the head is saying, "I want nothing to do with it."'

33
Computer admin: The class teacher

In the early days of computerized administration, classroom teachers developed a healthily cynical attitude to it. What it meant for them, after all, was that the head was always disappearing off on training sessions instead of coming down the corridor to teach. And just to add insult to injury, the secretary was also considerably less available than formerly. At some time in the unspecified future, all this would lead to big advantages for the teacher and the children. Or so they said.

It does take a long time for IT gains to work through a whole institution and there is a long and painful period during which things are actually more difficult rather than less. For example, introducing computerized registration usually means that for a time teachers are running the old manual system alongside the new one, because the data is too important to put at risk. Similarly, the introduction of computerized reporting to parents inevitably runs up against unforeseen snags which call for lots of patience and several meetings.

Piloting the school through all of this calls for determination and good management. Through it all, class teachers have the right to expect that they will be kept informed and consulted. In the end, though, there should be real benefits. Here is a list of some of the gains that staff should see from computerized administration. If they are inordinately slow to appear, then teachers have every right to stick a hand up at the next staff meeting and ask why.

- Computerized registration software (whatever the method of data collection) makes session and lesson registration easier, helps the tutor to follow up absences, and completely abolishes the task of adding up totals and working out percentages.

- A finance and budgeting package ought to mean that teachers and heads of departments are more aware of how much money they have to spend. They should also find that their requests for books and equipment are being met more quickly as orders are passed electronically to suppliers.
- Management and timetabling software make it much easier to start up a big school at the beginning of the school year. The timetable should start in earnest on Day One, with none of those 'dead' days that could last up to a week.
- The time-consuming chore of handling examination entries and results is reduced to almost nothing. Results, in particular, appear quickly and can be tabulated and analysed in all sorts of ways.
- National Curriculum assessment recording becomes a 'one-shot' operation. No teacher should have to copy data by hand from one place to another, or do any manual calculations.
- If staff are ready to accept 'statement banks' – and not all are – then nobody needs to write end of term reports any more. Even if they do want to write their own comments, reporting software substantially reduces the amount of time involved.
- Cover for absence is handled more efficiently and more fairly, and 'protected' free periods are more sacrosanct.
- Up-to-date class lists, in alphabetical or age order, with no inked-in deletions or additions, are available on demand.
- Standard letters about matches, concerts, PTA events are all available at short notice.
- Such publications as concert programmes and newsletters can be done more quickly and look a lot better.

Not every school will be able to offer all of these things. However, on the basis that the overwhelming majority of schools now have at least the beginnings of a management system, then many of them should be visible.

Beyond all of these functions – which are fairly standard, and have been available for a long time – lie other possibilities for the class teacher. One example is data handling on staffroom or classroom terminals. At the moment, in most schools, teachers interact with the computer system at second hand, often through the school office.

Data entry – for assessment or registration on SIMS, for example – is often done on an optical mark reader form, which is read at a central point. There is, though, the possibility of bringing terminals within reach so that teachers can have direct access. Ernest Clarke's 'SPARRC' (Software for Planning, Assessing, Recording and Reporting in the Classroom), for example, is designed so that a class teacher can record assessments on the classroom machine. Bromcom's RadioEARS gives each teacher a small computer which, although primarily intended for registration, has a much wider potential.

Another approach is to make standard laptops widely available, with word processing or admin software. How far one can go down the road of putting teachers in direct contact with admin software is limited partly by the willingness of teachers to do it. Some will take the view that sitting at a keyboard is not part of the job. Others will look at it differently. This is a management issue that many schools will have to face at some point.

Another limitation is to do with the Data Protection Act. If, for instance, you put the central admin system on a very wide network, then although there are levels of access, with passwords, given the interrelationship of some of the information, it's not always possible to give everyone exactly the rights they want.

One former head recalled an example of this.

'I put a terminal in the staffroom, for teachers to look at pupil data, but I made sure that only one particular area of the admin system was available. Even that was a problem, because not only were the timetable and address accessible but also details of emergency contact. One member of staff challenged me over whether that breached the Act. I think there are issues there. The principle of the Act is that computerized information should only be available to those with a right to know. Every terminal should have the eight principles of the Act on display by it.'

34

Computer admin: The school secretary

The job of school secretary has traditionally been, to say the least, multifaceted. There is soothing of aggrieved neighbours ('Thirty years I've lived here and never . . .'), of disgruntled teachers ('That MAN!') or of highly dudgeoned pupils ('It weren't me, Miss!'). Other jobs have included first aid, looking after visitors, collecting dinner money, answering the phone. Something new and complicated was not, on the whole, what they were looking for, and when information technology appeared in school offices in the late 1980s, the fear was that many secretaries would simply leave, taking years of experience and knowledge with them.

Inevitably, there were some who did go. On the whole, though, the local authority people who trained the secretaries were very impressed with their ability and enthusiasm. John Walker, who led Staffordshire's training, started by fearing the worst and was pleasantly surprised. 'We were told that we'd face wholesale resistance. In fact, they were quick to learn.'

His experience, and that of others, is that information technology, rather than driving secretaries away, has boosted their self-esteem by providing them with a very visible area of expertise which they can master and own. And in very many cases, stereotypical preconceptions about which school secretaries would take to computers and which would not have been entirely confounded.

What this means, to cut through the circumlocutions, is that if you thought female secretaries over forty would be slow to learn about computers, then you would be wrong in a very big way. The response of a Leicestershire village school secretary, who was in the throes of computer training, illustrates the point. 'I've worked here for twenty-four years, and I realized I either had to learn the system or give up my job, so I settled down to learn it. Now I find it very satisfying.'

Barbara Lennon, a long-serving middle school secretary in Warwickshire, has the same sort of story to tell. 'Computers changed my life completely. When I started here I just answered the phone and typed the occasional letter. I even had some time to work in classrooms with the children.'

Then along came the computerized management system. 'I started by thinking that I couldn't do it, but that was just a momentary thing really. I then saw it as a challenge, and now I quite enjoy using it. It's a shift of status, too, although I do miss the opportunity to get into the classroom. I don't have the contact with the children any more.'

Her main problem – which she shares with most other secretaries – is that there is simply no opportunity in the school day in which to sit quietly and find out what the software will do. 'There's just a lack of time to play around with the system.'

There is, of course, a recognizable irony in the fact that Mrs Lennon now, after having been given thousands of pounds' worth of efficiency-enhancing equipment, has less time than she had before.

Her transformation, in fact, from someone who was able to use her needlecraft expertise with groups of children into an administrative officer operating at an altogether higher level of expertise is symbolic of what has happened to primary schools since 1988 – and it would be a mistake to think that nothing has been lost along the way.

At secondary level, absorbing IT into the office has sometimes been easier simply because there was often more than one secretary already, and it was possible for people to develop specialisms in, say, finance or attendance monitoring.

One of the issues that arises from the enhanced status of the school secretary is that of whether schools pay them enough. Secretaries who are trained and experienced in word processing may well be only staying on in schools because they like the surroundings and the hours of work – which means, suggests John Walker, 'that to some extent we've been exploiting their skill and dedication'.

35

Computers in the small primary school

The big secondary school has an obvious need for computerized administration. The case for equipping the small primary school office with computers is less obvious, however. Gerald Haigh discusses this issue here.

On the staff notice board in a school which I recently visited was the playground duty rota. It read, simply, 'Mon – Liz: Tue – Pat: Wed – Clive: Thur – Liz: Fri – Pat.'

'I take it,' I said to the head, 'that with just three teachers, you don't feel the need for a sophisticated staff database?'

So far as computerizing the office goes, this just about sums up the issue for primary schools. Do you need electronic registration if you have fewer than a hundred pupils? Is it worth putting the accounts on computer when the sums involved are so small?

As Cambridgeshire primary head Graham Lockwood puts it, 'If you're discussing whether to use an attendance module, then if you have seventy-five pupils it's probably not an issue for you. With 400, though, it will be a real bonus.'

Often, in the early days of local management, when authorities were introducing admin packages to their schools, it was proposed that small schools would not need them. Surely a good paper system would do perfectly well?

This county hall logic, reasonable though it seemed, was doomed from the start, partly because it seriously underestimated the extent to which computers would be used, by even the smallest schools, for modelling budgets and for pupil assessment and reporting. It also took no account of the way that heads and governors in any sector of schooling will oppose anything that threatens to cut them off from the educational mainstream. Whatever the practicalities, if the IT revolution was happening, they wanted in.

John Walker, supporter of admin IT in Staffordshire, also feels that 'Apart from anything else, there were implications for promotion. Small school heads applying for bigger schools would not have the experience of computerized systems. A whole bunch of heads would be disenfranchised from IT. Usually, that was enough to convince the doubters.'

Whether the primary heads want the same system as the secondary schools, though, is still open to argument. They assume, rightly or wrongly, that admin systems were designed for secondary schools and are now being handed down to the primaries. Local management, after all, started in the secondary schools, and the software pioneers were usually secondary teachers.

Some suppliers try to address this feeling by providing different systems for primary and secondary. The particular requirements of the primary school, for instance, include the ability to show whether a pupil is full or part time; to include pupils below statutory school age; to print separate year groups when classes have mixed ages.

You have to work at any computerized administration system – spending both time and money – before it starts to reward you. It can be particularly difficult to do this in a primary school, which may well have a teaching head and part-time secretary. Bedfordshire primary head David Tuck believes that the answer is just to get on and do it. 'When we started with a new thing – attendance, for example – we sent the secretary into my room to learn the module without interruption, having someone else in to take the phone calls. You have to make time to do it.'

The same line of reasoning has led some primary heads to opt out of local authority 'travelling bursar' schemes. On the face of it, there is a lot of sense in allowing primaries to buy a share of an officer who stops by with a laptop to run the finance package. After all, this allows the head – who often lays claim to being 'a teacher first' – to pay attention to the curriculum matters from which he or she resents being diverted.

This is undoubtedly how some heads see it. Others, though, have decided that they want total ownership of the admin system. Leicestershire head Chris Davis puts a common point of view. 'We certainly appreciated our bursar, but we learned a lot more when she left and we had to do it ourselves.'

In the end, there is probably no alternative to employing more support staff. Right from the beginning of local management, most primary heads saw that they had either to upgrade their secretaries, or to increase their hours, or to take on somebody to help. Wherever it was possible – and surprisingly often it was – they did all three.

The costs are not all to do with people. Hardware has to be kept up to date, which means keeping a budget heading for the purpose. There can be pressure to revamp the building, too, as computers, printers, fax machines and optical mark readers are shipped into primary school offices designed for a part-time secretary with a telephone, a typewriter and a first aid kit. As a result, many primary schools have made increased office accommodation a priority.

In some cases the extra space has been achieved by reducing the size of the head's room. At St Giles School in North Warwickshire, for example, the head has done a straight room swap with the office staff. At Kilmorie Primary in Lewisham, a similar problem is being addressed by converting the rooms of the head, deputy and secretary into one open-plan space, and providing a small private room for the head or deputy to use as necessary.

All of this, added to the myriad other jobs that primary heads and secretaries have to do, means that primary schools have been slow to see the benefits of computerized systems. In many of them now, though, things are beginning to take off. Features such as the ability to complete DFE returns in minutes rather than days, or to have continuously updated pupil lists on tap, or to share 'what if we did this' budget models with the governors, or to handle correspondence more quickly and more professionally, are winning converts.

There is a real need, though, for a final word of caution. Perhaps because of all the pressures and doubts, together with a lack of an information technology tradition, primary schools are often poor at managing the security of their computer systems. A year or two ago, the National Council for Educational Technology (NCET) 'found no primary schools with systems which would have been able to survive theft, fire or computer failure'. Things may be improving now, but there are undoubtedly very many schools which simply do not, for example, take copies of saved data off the school site. As one head of an arson-attacked school put it, 'It's very much once bitten twice shy. We had to put every bit of data in all over again, and it's not something I ever want to repeat.'

36

Electronic data transfer

Computer-held data can be exchanged by sending floppy disks through the post, or it can be sent more quickly down the telephone line. Are school offices making full use of data exchange? Gerald Haigh asks the question and seeks some answers.

The concept of 'computers talking to each other' has become matter-of-fact reality, and teachers are busy exploring whether, and how, the Internet can help with learning.

In the school office, however, things are less clear. The management information system collects and handles a mass of pupil, staff and financial information. To what extent, though, does it need to talk to the world outside?

The most obvious useful link, for a local authority school, is with the finance department in the education office. Because financial tasks are split between school and authority, there has to be a frequent exchange of information. Very many schools, for example, still receive each month from the authority a paper printout from the mainframe, containing a long list of transactions each single one of which has to be compared with the school's own records.

This laborious paper exercise is, in fact, usually unnecessary in the sense that a good school finance package – SIMS, for example, or Key Solutions – is perfectly capable of doing the comparisons automatically. It will flag up only the non-matching items – the book that has been invoiced and apparently not ordered; the supply teacher whose pay claim has been miscoded – so that the school can deal with them. What usually stands in the way is the need to persuade the authority's mainframe computer to produce its information in the right way. Where this has been done – in Essex, for example – the saving in time in schools is very significant.

For this to happen, the link between the school computer and the authority does not, of course, have to be electronic. A floppy disk in the post does perfectly well – Essex worked like this for some time. The electronic link, though, quite apart from being quicker and less susceptible to loss and damage, is a lot cheaper for the authority. According to Chris Holder, technical manager of SIMS Support in Essex, 'It costs less than one call unit per school – the cost of telephone charges for twelve months is less than the cost of postage was for one month.'

Essex SIMS Support uses the same system to provide a link between schools and the examination boards. The examination boards, in fact, pioneered electronic document interchange in education. The then Midlands Examination Board (now MEG) was up and running by 1988, both receiving entries from schools and transferring results back. Chris Lyon, who chairs the EDI Coordination group at MEG, explained that 'It saves us a lot of keying and also we tend to get better quality data – there's no misinterpretation of miles of Tipp-Exed paper!'

In the West Midlands Office of MEG (Midland Examining Group), ninety-three per cent of entries are received electronically from schools and colleges (a small amount of this is on disk, but most is down the phone line). This Board also makes extensive use of the link for exchanging electronic mail with schools – a great help, pointed out Chris Lyon, to teachers who find it difficult to make telephone calls during the working day. This also makes it possible to give an official response, at very short notice, in a way that would not be acceptable by telephone. For example, said Chris Lyon, 'One school had a child turn up for an exam who had mistakenly not been entered. The person in charge sent a message across to us and by the time the exam was started they had the authorization that he could be accepted as a candidate.'

Schools and authorities are also exploring electronic mail links, school to authority and school to school. If a link is already in place for financial data, for example, it makes sense to exploit it for other messages. In a number of cases, though, these systems have been under-used, usually because they have been too unwieldy for hard-pressed heads and part-time secretaries to bother with. In Devon, for example, a mainframe messaging system was found to be too slow and also too expensive in telephone time, because messages had to be composed and received during connection.

Devon, therefore, has for a year been piloting a more user-friendly electronic mail system for Windows – BeyondMail. The pilot has thrown up some interesting issues – the need, for example, to keep control of junk mail. In Devon, according to the report of the pilot project, 'Schools found they were getting pointless messages relating to County Hall staff ... about parking, security of handbags, Christmas decorations, etc.' A filter is now in place, but the issue of how to prevent important items becoming lost among trivial ones is there for all such systems. If it is not controlled, many people simply stop looking.

The Devon schools also wanted adequate training, though they found that half a day was enough for this system. BeyondMail is clearly going to be an asset to Devon schools, not least because the authority uses it to offer schools a way into the Internet at reasonable cost, and links have already been established between Devon and schools in Canada and the USA.

Electronic communication is going to grow. Already, in those authorities which either have no electronic mail or only an unwieldy internal system, there is pressure for something more accessible. Chris Holder in Essex told me that 'Schools are very keen to be able to have e-mail into local firms and to their governors, perhaps directly to the person they want in the authority. I think that will take us down the Internet route.'

Peter Williams of Key Solutions, who is talking to user authorities about electronic data transfer, foresees that 'In five years the advanced school office will probably be doing all its ordering via electronic transfer (some suppliers already have electronic catalogues), perhaps doing bank payments. Then there's the whole area of transfer of pupil records between schools and between local authorities.'

Part Five
Managing Finance

37

Thirteen money-savers

Schools faced with having to make budget savings tend, under-standably, to look at major budget headings, such as staffing. The feeling among heads and governors is that other budget areas are insignificant by comparison, and that, therefore, there is little point in wasting time on them.

That this might not be so is set out here by Bob Doe, whose thirteen money-saving suggestions are based on a report produced for the Association for Teachers and Lecturers by a leading personnel consultant. Schools should, he says:

- Thoroughly review all administrative functions, cutting out all inessential work, improving bureaucratic procedures, making better use of information technology or administrative staff, more part-time non-teaching staff and better management of service supply arrangements.
- Simplify work systems or procedures: streamlining the number of stages in a procedure; cutting out duplication of effort, bottle-necks or unnecessarily detailed checking or 'references up'.
- Improve efficiency through better equipment, balancing the initial costs of improved information technology equipment against the measurable savings through increased efficiency of staff. This could not only improve efficiency of accountancy work but also save time and effort on pupil records, electronic mail, timetabling, word processing and storage of documents.
- Reduce non-productive time, analysing how much time staff spend on different activities to ensure time is utilized effectively. Larger secondary schools may be able to cut out interdepart-mental delays and time spent on internal co-ordination but there is less likely to be scope for such savings in small primaries.

- Introduce de-layering, simplifying organizational structures by removing complete levels or layers of management to shorten the links between top management and front-line staff, and devolving decision making closer to the point where the decisions are implemented and saving on management over-heads. If deputy heads are paid more to assist the head with non-teaching duties, why do they spend 100 per cent of their time in the classroom in about a third of all primary schools? Paying deputy salaries for little or no non-teaching managerial work raises questions about the cost-effective use of salary budgets. Larger schools with more than one deputy should ask if they all need to be paid on deputy salary scales.

- Enable professionals to work more effectively by transferring their non-professional work to cheaper staff. Some deputy heads spend too much time on minor administrative functions which could be transferred to clerical staff. Classroom assistants generally improve the effectiveness of teachers rather than offer scope for economies.

- Improve employee competence, increasing productivity through training. Better management training for heads, in-service training for teachers and training in information technology and administrative processes for school secretaries would improve efficiency in the long term but would have initial costs and would not contribute to rapid savings.

- Motivate staff to work better or harder. However, the report suggests that performance-related pay will not do this, because the majority of teachers are already highly motivated and doing more than meet their basic contractual obligations.

- Investigate scope for greater flexibility in the hours of administrative and support staff. When caretakers are required to be on duty out of school time, rescheduling their working hours can save on overtime costs.

- Employ staff on other forms of contract than full-time and open-ended for work which is spasmodic, unpredictable or short-term. Consider term-time appointments only for clerical staff and part-time work for admin staff. Increasing use of part-time teachers raises questions of effectiveness, equal opportunities (most are women) and equal pay.

- Seek more cost-effective arangements for buying in goods and services, possibly through tenders or consortium arrangements with other schools.

- Reduce expenditure on services. Control spending on fuel, telephones, water and postage by introducing economy measures (insulation, turning down the thermostat, fitting time controls, telephone monitoring and barring certain numbers) and checking invoice details.
- Manage premises more efficiently – look at use of space and draw up plans for building maintenance. Use caretakers for simple repairs and volunteers for decoration.

Bob Doe is Deputy Editor of the *Times Educational Supplement*.

38
Leasing

The business world is familiar with the concept of leasing, which allows large items of equipment to be, in effect, hired. The obvious advantage is that it avoids the need to eat into capital funds.

Schools are less accustomed to leasing, partly because until recently major equipment was bought by the local authority, and partly because there are rules governing the way that schools can use leasing and other forms of deferred payment. Recently, though, leasing firms have been working to convince schools of the wisdom of leasing. In this article Gerald Haigh looks at some of the advantages and disadvantages.

If I say to you, 'For ten bob you can borrow my bike for a fortnight', then the arrangement is surely very clear. You know perfectly well that you have not bought my bike. What you have bought is the right to use it. The bike is still mine, as you would rapidly discover were you to lose it, give it away or bend the front wheel in the tramlines. At the end of the fortnight, the bike must come back to me in good nick – and if all has gone well we might extend the arrangement, although we would probably renegotiate the fee.

This, effectively, is what leasing is – paying for the use of expensive equipment that either you cannot afford or that you simply do not want to spend good money on at the moment.

In the business world, leasing is an old and familiar friend. Firms lease just about anything from hot air hand dryers to whole fleets of vehicles. Eighty-five of the Times Top 100 companies lease equipment.

Schools, though, have up to now been slow to get into leasing. Governors are notoriously careful with their budgets, as has been shown by all the stories about large unspent end-of-year surpluses, and schools are not, as individuals are, free to run up unmanageable debts. Most of them are publicly accountable institutions, subject to both national and local regulations about the way they handle their money. Grant-maintained schools, particularly, are subject to careful regulation when it comes to raising credit, and local authority schools are bound by local government finance rules.

Nevertheless, more and more schools are beginning to wonder whether they really do need to wait for that new computer system, trying to build up a fund only to see it raided when some emergency comes along. At William Parker School in Hastings, for example, leasing has allowed the school to have its office computer system, a booklet maker, Archimedes computers for classroom use and a vacuum former for the technology department – many thousands of pounds' worth of equipment that the school could not possibly have afforded to buy outright. Similarly, Cranleigh, an independent HMC school, has on lease two sophisticated photocopiers, a postage franking machine and the school telephone system. The photocopiers alone would have cost a total of over eighty thousand pounds to buy and the obvious point, as Nicholas North, Cranleigh's Deputy Bursar, pointed out, is 'that it eases the cash flow problems'.

Another advantage, Mr North explained, is that because you do not own the equipment, you are not left with it when it becomes obsolete – which is why the school is leasing its phone system. 'Technology is moving forward all the time.'

At William Parker, Dr Bob Megit, head of resources, said that 'It does solve the short-term problem. With computers, for example, they are going to be obsolete anyway in five years, so you can write them off and start again.'

Both Mr North and Dr Megit, however, were clear that a school going in for leasing had to know what questions to ask. Mr North, for example, suggests looking carefully at the length of time you are signing up for. 'I'd definitely be wary about going too far into the future.'

Mr North also warned against automatically renewing a lease. 'The other day the person dealing with my franking machine came in and asked me to sign up for another five years, but I said I had decided to step back and see what else is on the market.'

One benefit of this, he has found, is that the firms you approach then compete with each other. 'I've saved quite a lot of money pitching one against the other.'

Your leased equipment usually belongs not to the firm who delivered it but to the leasing company, which has bought the machine from the manufacturer and is leasing it to you. This means that you do not necessarily have to deal with the leasing firm that comes as part of the rep's package. You can very easily go to an independent leasing company who will buy the equipment you need and then lease it to you.

Rebecca Hunt, of Biddenham Asset Finance, believes that 'Using leasing companies which work independently from equipment suppliers allows lessees to choose the equipment which best suits their requirements.'

A school looking at buying a piece of equipment can, she explained, 'either come to us first and then go shopping with the finance, or they can look at the equipment first and then see if we are happy to finance it'.

What, I wondered, were the questions that schools ought to ask? Cost, presumably, was one issue 'Percentages – flat rates and APRs – aren't easy to compare. They're very much affected by up-front payments – whether there's a deposit or not; whether payments are made quarterly, annually, in advance or in arrears. The best way is to compare the cost per thousand pounds borrowed.'

Cost per thousand means that, for example, a firm that quoted £23.27 per thousand (a typical figure mentioned by Rebecca Hunt) on a five thousand pound IT system would want £116.35 a month for five years – a total of £6,981.

'Some firms have standardized rates,' explained Rebecca Hunt, 'but we try to look at the strength of each proposal and tailor the rate to it.'

Schools should, she warned, watch out for documentation charges, and also ask what would happen if interest rates were to change. 'You need to know also whether you are dealing with a principal or a broker. A broker may add on their own commission charges.'

Most importantly, though, urged Rebecca Hunt, 'Seek independent advice – local authority schools should go to their authority. Others should go to their financial advisers, and there is the Consumer Credit Trade Association.'

And last but not least, schools should not, of course, get carried away to the point where their leasing bill is a worrying burden. School budgets are determined by pupil numbers, and these can sometimes unexpectedly change, leaving a school still having to find – for up to five years – the monthly leasing payment from a shrinking balance.

Biddenham Asset Finance, Seckloe House, 101 North Thirteenth Street, Central Milton Keynes, Buckinghamshire MK9 3NU

CCTA, Tennyson House, 159–163 Great Portland Street, London W1M 5FD

39

Capital replacement

Heads and governors are often still unsure how to plan for capital replacement. They also are sometimes guilty of allowing large unspent balances to build up year by year. Here, Brian Knight argues for a more planned approach to capital replacement.

School budget surpluses are an embarrassment. They give politicians the notion that schools have more money than they need. They appear to soften the impact of budget cuts this year and so encourage similar cuts next year. They tie up funds that should be used productively. They imply unthinking financial management. Surpluses cannot be justified unless they have a specific identified purpose. So, what is justifiable?

- A development fund for a specific identified project
- A bridging fund to bridge across a trough between two funding peaks, e.g. caused by a dip in enrolment
- A contingency fund for possible problems (but not a large unallocated surplus)
- A capital replacement fund.

If your present surpluses had been allocated this way, school planning would be more explicit and our present embarrassment would be less.

Of these, the most neglected function – but the most important one in the long term – is the capital replacement fund.

Schools are becoming more capital-intensive by the day. The emphasis upon science and technology in the National Curriculum, the application of information technology across the range of subjects, improvements in reprographics and computerization of school offices all require more capital equipment and give us a glimpse of what schools may become in the information age.

Yet few schools make any measured allowance for capital replacement. Pre-local management, they did not need to do so – they only had to hope that Auntie LEA would provide. Even local authorities did not make calculated allowance for depreciation. There was often, in good times at least, a capital replacement fund or 'central fund' which met the most urgent pleas from the school. But now such funds have dried up, and schools have to provide from their own budgets. Most do not – often because they feel there is no slack for such a luxury. But even those that could create a replacement fund do not do so, probably because depreciation is still an unfamiliar concept.

Technically, depreciation is the decline in value of an asset over time. For example, furniture bought in year 1 may last ten years, and so may be thought of as being consumed over that period until it needs replacement. So depreciation required an accounting convention for writing off the book value of capital assets on a balance sheet, often on a percentage basis.

However, state schools do not produce balance sheets – unlike, for example, the locally managed schools in New Zealand, which account annually for their assets with allowance for depreciation. And schools still have to pay the whole cost of the purchase in year 1, unless they lease it. At the time of writing, they are not yet able to borrow for capital spending, paying for it in debt charges.

The accountant's approach to depreciation is a useful management tool, although it has little appeal for schools at present. It highlights the true cost of capital replacement, even if the school cannot make proper allowance for it, and so reveals the schools' true operating costs. Without a calculation for depreciation, replacement needs are underestimated. For example, some schools are now finding that their BBC computers are becoming obsolete.

City technology colleges originally argued strongly that provision for depreciation of buildings and equipment should be included in their annual grants from the Department for Education. Presumably the CTC's sponsors saw this as normal commercial practice. It also mirrored the practice of independent schools, who typically allow for depreciation on a full cost basis within their accounts, or by adjustment to fee levels. But the argument cut no ice with the DFE, which like LEAs had not been accustomed to regular capital replacement (and was no doubt horrified by the financial implications). Grant-maintained schools raised a similar argument, also in vain.

Yet it is no good schools just hoping that something will turn up. That is the Mr Micawber theory of financial management. Capital equipment will depreciate and logically allowance should be made for this.

First we need to estimate depreciation systematically. So an inventory of the school's capital assets is needed. These are likely to include information technology, office, reprographics and audio-visual equipment; science, technology, art, music and PR equipment; furniture, furnishings and fittings such as blackout; school vehicles; playing fields equipment and furniture. GM schools will also be responsible for the fabric of their buildings.

The next step is to assess annual replacement costs. A proforma can be used for this (see the simple example in Table 39.1). This calculates the replacement value and mean life left for each item on the inventory and so the annual replacement costs which can then be aggregated for the whole inventory. A spreadsheet can make these calculations and its updating is quite straightforward.

Identifying replacement needs is one thing – funding them is quite another. There are several possible strategies:

- Set aside a sum for capital replacement each year in the school budget. This is fine if the budget is buoyant, but under pressure it may be the first thing to go. Some items may be too expensive for a single year's budget.
- Create a capital replacement fund, fed with annual sums corresponding to the total current annual replacement costs as calculated above. This averages out peaks and troughs, and puts replacement on a more regular footing. But it is only worthwhile if the interest the school can earn on the fund is greater than inflation.

  There is also the risk that the capital replacement fund could be raided in extremities. However, it could be a better use for balances which many schools still roll forward each year. Converting these to capital replacement funds would make them more purposeful and politically acceptable.
- Live from year to year, coping with demands as they arise. This is what most schools do. It has the merit of judging each capital replacement demand against all other priorities, and it is less

work. But it is really hand-to-mouth budgeting, exposed to the problems outlined earlier.

My own view about capital replacement has changed. I used to think that it was unrealistic to require such an element within a budget, as schools historically had never provided for it, and most did not have the budget flexibility to do so. However, that now seems a head-in-the-sand policy. Capital replacement will grow steadily in importance, and it is crucial that schools make provision for it.

If that provision isn't enough – and usually it will be far from enough – the school should flag up this 'capital replacement gap' as boldly as possible. Governors, parents, the electorate, the Department of Education and even the government need to realize that schools are now climbing on to a new plateau of capital expenditure. That means ear-marked capital replacement funds – not unallocated and eminently disposable surpluses.

Brian Knight is an honorary research fellow of the University of Exeter, an educational consultant and author of *Financial Management for Schools: The Thinking Manager's Guide* (Heinemann, £14.00, ISBN 0 435 804812).

Table 39.1 *Calculations of capital replacement cost*

Item	Quantity	Replacement value	Total replacement value (a × b)	Life from new (years)	Date bought	Life left (years)	Annual replacement cost (c/f)
	a	b	c	d	e	f	
TV	1	400	400	8	1991	4	100
Video	2	300	600	10	1989	4	150
Computer	4	1000	4000	8	1989	2	2000
Computer	4	1000	4000	8	1995	8	500
Epidiascope	1	Not to be replaced					2750

40

Ten questions to ask the bank

Schools are increasingly taking the option of running their own bank accounts, and paying their own bills rather than passing them to the local authority. Unsurprisingly, therefore, banks are interested in winning business from schools. Equally unsurprisingly, not all bankers are familiar with what schools need. So, if you are having trouble choosing between the listening bank, the action bank or any of the others, here from Anat Arkin are ten questions to put to local bank managers.

1 Does your bank have a scheme specially designed for schools? Some high street banks do. Others prefer to say that they treat every business, of whatever kind, on its own merits. Some banks, too, seem keener on attracting business from the grant-maintained sector than from local authority schools, which do not normally handle the money used to pay teachers' salaries.

2 What experience do you have of working with schools? You will not always get a straight answer to this. They may refuse to disclose information about their share of the schools or any other market, while some of the biggest banks say they do not list schools as a separate category in their databases.

   The local branch manager's own experience of working with schools is probably just as important as the bank's share of the market, so find out if other schools hold accounts there and if the manager knows anything about school finances. A bank manager who is also a local school governor could be a good choice.

3 Will we earn interest on a current account? Check and compare

the details. You need to know not only the rate of interest, but the threshold balance above which interest will be paid, and whether there are higher interest rates for larger balances.

A bank which does not pay interest on a current account may, however, offer a 'sweep' facility by which current account funds above a certain level are switched into interest-earning deposit accounts.

4 Can you handle our payroll? If your school is responsible for its own payroll administration, most banks will offer to do it – at a price. All you have to do is provide a list of staff and payment information including deductions and pay increases. There is often a minimum charge for this service, which can make it prohibitively expensive for small schools. You might, however, think about pooling budgets with other schools and sharing the costs of payroll and other administrative services.

5 Do you offer electronic banking? Linking your computer to the bank's computer enables you to keep track of funds, monitor balances and switch funds between accounts to get the best return. It also does away with the need for frequent trips to the bank – but, again, this facility and the technology to support it can be expensive. An alternative is a telephone banking service. This enables schools to use a tone-generating telephone or a tonepad to access their accounts at any time.

6 What bank charges will we have to pay? Bank charges vary, with the best deals often coming as packages of services. Some banks offer free cheque book accounts to schools so long as accounts are kept in credit. Check on other free services, such as commission-free currency exchanges for trips abroad.

7 What happens to the money we deposit? If you are worried that your school's funds will be invested in tobacco manufacture, factory farming, or other activity that your school might find offensive, you are probably best off banking with the Co-op. But look carefully at the bank's much-vaunted ethical policy. If you object to all experiments on animals, you may not be entirely reassured by the Co-op's promise not to invest in businesses involved in animal experimentation for cosmetic purposes. The bank also says it will not finance the manufacture or sale of arms – but only to 'any country which has an oppressive regime'.

Some of the other banks are also waking up to customers' concerns about the way their money is used, although the most one high street bank can say is that it does not knowingly do business with drug-runners or money launderers. Some may go further, and offer schools the chance to specify areas in which they do not want to place their investments.

8 Do you always get your sums right? A survey by the Consumers' Association found that one in seven bank and building society customers surveyed had had money incorrectly taken from their account and one in eight had been charged incorrectly.

The survey also showed high levels of dissatisfaction with information on charges and interest rates. Although the survey looked at the experience of personal rather than business customers, you might want to consider what it found about the branch you are considering for your school.

9 What about banking services for staff? Banks will usually offer potential banking services to the staff of schools holding accounts with them. These services can range from interest-bearing current accounts to personal loans at favourable interest rates. Some banks will also give free advice on pensions, savings and things like insurance.

10 What is my next step? Don't rush into any decisions. Shop around and talk to as many bank managers as you can before committing your school to an important relationship that could last for years.

Anat Arkin is a freelance writer.

Index